PARAGON
ISSUES IN
PHILOSOPHY

PARAGON ISSUES IN PHILOSOPHY

THE PARAGON ISSUES IN PHILOSOPHY SERIES

At colleges and universities, interest in the traditional areas of philosophy remains strong. Many new currents flow within them, too, but some of these—the rise of cognitive science, for example, or feminist philosophy—went largely unnoticed in undergraduate philosophy courses until the end of the 1980s. The Paragon Issues in Philosophy Series responds to both perennial and newly influential concerns by bringing together a team of able philosophers to address the fundamental issues in philosophy today and to outline the state of contemporary discussion about them.

More than twenty volumes are scheduled; they are organized into three major categories. The first covers the standard topics—metaphysics, theory of knowledge, ethics, and political philosophy—stressing innovative developments in those disciplines. The second focuses on more specialized but still vital concerns in the philosophies of science, religion, history, sport, and other areas. The third category explores new work that relates philosophy and fields such as feminist criticism, medicine, economics, technology, and literature.

The level of writing is aimed at undergraduate students who have little previous experience studying philosophy. The books provide brief but accurate introductions that appraise the state of the art in their fields and show how the history of thought about their topics developed. Each volume is complete in itself but also complements others in the series.

Traumatic change characterizes these last years of the twentieth century: all of it involves philosophical issues. The editorial staff at Paragon House has worked with us to develop this series. We hope it will encourage the understanding needed in our times, which are as complicated and problematic as they are promising.

John K. Roth   Frederick Sontag
Claremont McKenna College   Pomona College

PHILOSOPHY
AND
FEMINIST
CRITICISM

ALSO BY EVE BROWNING COLE

EXPLORATIONS IN FEMINIST ETHICS: Theory and Practice
(co-edited with Susan Coultrap—McQuin)
Indiana University Press, 1992.

EVE BROWNING COLE

The University of Minnesota
at Duluth

PHILOSOPHY
AND
FEMINIST
CRITICISM
AN INTRODUCTION

PARAGON
ISSUES IN
PHILOSOPHY

PARAGON HOUSE • NEW YORK

FIRST EDITION, 1993

PUBLISHED IN THE UNITED STATES BY
PARAGON HOUSE
90 FIFTH AVENUE
NEW YORK, N.Y. 10011

COPYRIGHT © 1993 BY PARAGON HOUSE

LIBRARY OF CONGRESS CATALOGING-IN-PUBLICATION DATA

Cole, Eve Browning
    Philosophy and feminist criticism / Eve Browning Cole. — 1st ed.
       p.   cm. — (Paragon issues in philosophy)
    Includes bibliographical references and index.
    ISBN 1-55778-457-4
    1. Feminist theory.   2. Feminist criticism.   3. Philosophy.
I. Title.   II. Series.
HQ1190.C65   1993
305.42'01—dc20   92-10720
                                                 CIP

MANUFACTURED IN THE UNITED STATES OF AMERICA

TO JULIE WARD, TAMAR RUDAVSKY,
AND PATRICIA CURD
WITH GRATITUDE FOR THE LAUGHTER
THAT SAVES OUR SANITY

CONTENTS

PREFACE

This book provides an introduction to feminist philosophy by describing *both* some of the ways in which feminist philosophers criticize traditional Western thought *and* some of the ways in which they are constructively contributing to new philosophical traditions. Since the activity of academic feminist philosophers, in the short time in which they have been teaching and publishing within the academy, has been intense and highly productive, this book is necessarily selective. The suggestions for further reading that conclude each chapter can, however, expand the scope of study for the interested reader.

Within the limits of the present book, I have attempted to convey to the reader some of the excitement of feminist philosophical work. This way of doing philosophy is in many respects new and many of the questions and debates are in formative states. The reader should feel invited to enter into feminist philosophy as into a welcoming room—one in which the furniture may be moved around from one day to the next but in which there is always a comfortable chair and a group of cheerful companions who look forward to hearing one's views. Enfranchisement, involvement, inclusion, and comradeship are foundational elements in feminism.

Although my goal has been to give a representative picture of the concerns and aims of feminist philosophers today, I am able to view these only from my own unavoidably limited perspective: that of a white, privileged, heterosexual Western woman with biases both conscious and unconscious. I have felt the severity of these perspectival limitations most seriously when writing about lesbian, black, and

American Indian feminist thought. But the desire to convey some of the beauty and power of these modes of philosophizing has motivated me to write of these groups of which I am not a member.

The term *philosophy* has at least two distinct families of meaning: in one, it denotes the heartfelt convictions of individuals and cultures, by which their lives are guided; in another, it signifies the professional and institutionalized project of academics (students and faculty) involved in a more or less stable curriculum, in publications in "reputable" journals, and so on. Feminist philosophers (in both senses) work toward a harmonizing of the two families of meaning. They lament the distance between a philosophy that can function as a guide to life and political action, on one side, and a philosophy that enjoys institutional prestige but is of little relevance outside the ivy-covered walls, on the other. In what follows, such terms as *institutionalized, academic, dominant, canonical,* and *mainstream* denote the philosophy of the professional philosophers, even though these terms are awkward. Where the term *philosophy* appears by itself, the context should make clear which sense, the narrower or the wider, is at stake.

I have dedicated this book to three dear friends, with whom I have discussed many of the issues raised herein and from each of whom I have learned more than I can say. Their wisdom, relentless honesty, and unfailing good humor have been a gift beyond all price, and their companionship in our shared struggle to bring the two senses of philosophy together for ourselves has been a blessing.

Eve Browning Cole
Duluth, Minnesota
February 1992

CHAPTER ONE

THE EMERGENCE OF FEMINIST PHILOSOPHY

I n a famous passage from the *Metaphysics*, Aristotle claims that
"Philosophy begins in wonder."[1] Aristotle goes on to explain that
the particular kind of intellectual activity philosophy represents can
find its beginnings only when the material needs of the philosopher-to-
be are largely satisfied and the mind can turn itself in a relaxed way to
reflective why-questions. He gives as an example the priestly class in
ancient Egypt, who were completely subsidized by the royal family
and thus able to think full-time in an atmosphere free from troubles and
mundane complications.

Feminist philosophy presents a stark contrast to the Aristotelian picture. Its emergence in the Western philosophical community during the
late 1960s and early 1970s was a direct response to real social movements and political problems; feminist philosophy begins, not in wonder, but in an intense political engagement such as would have totally
discombobulated the average Egyptian priest.

In a sense, of course, the Aristotelian picture has never been really
accurate concerning philosophy as a whole. Many philosophical movements have had their origin in political or economic struggle, and many
philosophers have been motivated by emotional attitudes far removed
from the detached bemusement Aristotle seems to have in mind. Nevertheless traditional philosophy has somehow retained its image as a
purely theoretical discipline, timeless, lofty and abstract, unsullied by
historical, temporal, or even personal concerns. Spinoza's call to view
nature *sub specie aeternitatis* — "under the aspect of eternity" — has
always seemed to many to encapsulate what it means to view some-

thing as a true philosopher. And it cannot be denied that the sweep of vision presented to a God's-eye view has a definite and powerful appeal.

But feminist philosophy calls us to the things of this world, and this call is a call for change. Thus feminist philosophers diverge from the traditional or stereotypical image of the philosopher in two ways: (1) They address themselves to particular historical situations, avoiding the flight into abstraction wherever possible; and (2) Their philosophical thinking is oriented toward a specific goal: the liberation of human beings from all forms of oppression, foremost among which stands the oppression of women; crossing race and class boundaries, spanning known history, gender injustice is the great constant of human experience.[2] It is a form of injustice of which traditional philosophy has been largely and perhaps willfully oblivious. Feminist philosophers have set themselves the task of dispelling that oblivion, by exploring its conceptual roots and transforming their discipline so that it can no longer lack sensitivity to real social injustice, and so that it will no longer be powerless to effect real social change. As the eradication of all forms of human oppression is the overarching goal of feminists, feminist philosophers devote their energies to this task as well, from the standpoint of a philosophy criticized and transformed.[3]

THE FIRST ISSUES

Although it is impossible to locate the beginnings of any movement in thought, because all such movements grow organically out of an infinitely complex network of conceptual and social influences, locating the origins of feminist philosophy is particularly difficult for several reasons. First, though most people tend to think of feminism as a quite modern or contemporary movement in thought, we can also point to important protofeminist philosophical essays written as far back as the eighteenth century. A second factor contributing to the difficulty of pinpointing origins for feminist philosophy has to do with the fact that important contributions have been and continue to be made through literary genres other than the traditional philosophical essay: speeches, short stories, plays, and novels. A full history of the early protofeminist essays along with the rhetorical and fictional contributing sources would be a huge undertaking, but in this section I will briefly introduce one representative from each group whose work is highly relevant to the concerns of this chapter.

Mary Wollstonecraft (1759–1797) wrote *A Vindication of the Rights of Men* as a response to Edmund Burke's *Reflections on the Revolution in France*, in which Burke had argued against the concepts that grounded the great political revolutions of the eighteenth century: universal human rights, liberty, equality, and fraternity. Burke believed that talk of equality can only bring unhappiness to those "destined to travel in the obscure walk of laborious life." And regarding women, he seems to have had decidedly negative views: "A woman is but an animal, and an animal not of the highest order."[4]

Mary Wollstonecraft's reply to Burke, published in 1790, is a spirited and closely reasoned defense of natural rights, followed in 1792 with *A Vindication of the Rights of Woman*, designed to address both the misogyny apparent in Burke's tract and the inconsistency in much of the natural-rights moral philosophy of the day. According to many philosophers, possession of full moral and political rights is based on the possession of reason; but the possession of reason is denied to women, therefore women do not possess full moral and political rights.

Wollstonecraft argued that the most significant gender differences in intellectual skills, temperament, and ethical values were products of socialization and education, rather than natural or biological facts:

Many are the causes that, in the present corrupt state of society, contribute to enslave women by cramping their understandings and sharpening their senses . . . [i]n the education of women, the cultivation of the understanding is always subordinate to the acquirement of some corporeal accomplishment; even while enervated by confinement and false notions of modesty, the body is prevented from attaining that grace and beauty which relaxed half-formed limbs never exhibit. Besides, in youth their faculties are not brought forward by emulation; and having no serious scientific study, if they have natural sagacity it is turned too soon on life and manners.[5]

Wollstonecraft's argument, perceived as scandalously radical in its day, proceeds along lines which have become quite familiar to us and which form the philosophical foundations of arguments for "equal opportunity" in education and in the workplace. Essentially, she maintains that we are in no position to claim that men and women are differentially equipped for any training or employment until we have allowed them to experience similar socialization and education processes. In the absence of comparative data based on egalitarian learning environments from earliest childhood, maintaining that men and women are intellectually and morally different can only reflect irrational prejudice, especially when this results in male privilege and the exclusion of women from spheres of activity and participation which they reasonably desire:

If [women] be really capable of acting like rational creatures, let them not be treated like slaves; or, like the brutes who are dependent on the reason of man, when they associate with him; but cultivate their minds, give them the salutary, sublime curb of principle, and let them attain conscious dignity by feeling themselves only dependent on God.[6]

Wollstonecraft's arguments are taken up in very similar form by John Stuart Mill over a century later[7] and are echoed in feminist arguments within the women's suffrage movements in England and the United States throughout the nineteenth and early twentieth centuries. She is thus, in a paradoxical way, both a relatively isolated voice in her own time and a powerful foundational source for subsequent thinkers and activists.[8]

Charlotte Perkins Gilman (1860–1935) was a prolific essayist, the author of many books on political economy and society, the editor of her own journal, and a novelist of considerable popularity. One of her most philosophical novels is a feminist utopian work entitled *Herland*, in which a band of male explorers encounter a society that consists only of women.[9] In describing the meeting between the explorers' expectations and the women's fictional social reality, Gilman provides a compelling and often hilarious feminist critique of contemporary American society. She also raises philosophical themes which have been integral to Euro-American feminist thought down to our own day.

The explorers are a heterogeneous group, and while one (described as a "romantic" and "a tender soul") expects the women's country to be "just blossoming with roses and babies and canaries and tidies, and all that sort of thing," another "had visions of a sort of sublimated summer resort—just Girls and Girls and Girls."[10] The third member of the group imagines a matriarchal society in which men are present but segregated, making what he chastely designates "an annual visit—a sort of wedding call" to the women's quarters.

All of them are completely mistaken, and the novel portrays the slow death of their misconceptions as they meet and become familiar with an all-female culture. Initially they are met at the border by a band of women all of whom are middle-aged; this in itself is a shock to the men. The narrator explains the men's surprise:

In all our discussions and speculations we had always unconsciously assumed that the women, whatever else they might be, would be young . . . "Woman" in the abstract is young and, we assume, charming. As they get older they pass off the stage, somehow, into private ownership mostly, or out of it altogether. But these good ladies were very much on the stage, and yet any one of them might have been a grandmother.[11]

This little scene makes, in a delicate and compact way, several significant points. It underscores the stereotypical qualities of the abstraction *woman*; this abstraction carries associations, such as "young" and "charming," which seem surprisingly displaced by the appearance of real members of the women's society. It also conveys, thanks to the narrator's engaging frankness, the idea that marriage (here designated "private ownership") is seen as the abandonment of the status "woman," as "leaving the stage" of life in a way only slightly less thoroughgoing than death (the state in which one is "out of it altogether").

The women's culture involves communal ownership of the means of production, the delegation of child care (conceived as the most important work of the society) to experts, a goddess-centered spirituality, universal enfranchisement and participatory democracy, and many other socialist–feminist concepts. The device of the confrontation between outsider males and the inhabitants of Herland enables Gilman to defend each of these concepts to a quizzical or downright skeptical audience, while the demand for credibility requires her to provide sufficient detail, explanation, and characterization to make the scenario live for the reader. Within this framework, Gilman's philosophical program achieves dramatic vitality while simultaneously defending itself rigorously. *Herland* is a quite deliberate employment of a fictional medium to deliver an argued feminist philosophical message.

The philosophical foundations from which Mary Wollstonecraft, on the one hand, and Charlotte Perkins Gilman, on the other, build their respective thought projects differ drastically and constitute the two most widely held and broadly opposed outlooks in feminist philosophy today. Wollstonecraft works within a framework of universal human rights, in which freedom of self-determination and individual autonomy or the capacity to direct one's own life are of paramount importance. Her ideal society is one in which each person possesses certain inalienable basic rights respected by every other person, according to a kind of rule of noninterference. "Liberty" is the right of each individual to behave as she or he wishes, legitimately limited only by the requirement not to interfere with the liberty of others. This is the political outlook known as *liberalism*, and Wollstonecraft is the first recognizable *liberal feminist*. Liberal feminism is widely represented in the Euro-American world today; its aims center around the achievement of equal opportunity between women and men: in education, in access to career opportunities, in compensation and advancement. Liberal feminists also strive to ensure women and men equal treatment under law, equal advantage under legislation and taxation, and equal opportunity for self-determination.

But how much social change is required in order to bring about all of these desired equalities? Here a vast amount of disagreement exists.

Some argue that the existing political/economic systems of the developed capitalist Western world are well suited more or less as they stand to provide gender equality; we must only weed out any accidental inequality-making mechanisms which have intruded themselves down through history (such as marriage laws which allowed husbands, but not wives, to file for divorce, or rape-prosecution procedures which indirectly place the victim on trial) and watch carefully to prevent abuses or distortions of the system (such as sexual harassment).

Others argue that this kind of reform is not extensive enough, for it does not get at the question of *how* the unfair laws and the abusive practices came to be in the first place. If we already live in a political system founded upon universal human rights and a deep commitment to individual liberty, how could such gender-imbalanced practices ever develop, much less be tolerated for years as "just the way things are"? Some liberal feminists respond by arguing that we really don't yet have a pure liberal democracy, any more than we have a purely capitalistic economy. Wollstonecraft might maintain that the gender-differentiated practices we find objectionable are evidence that, although our political foundation is sound, we have not yet built a completely stable and harmonious structure on its basis. Thus the task, for those interested in genuine equality, is to bring the superstructure into substantive coherence with its liberal base.

Others argue that the problem lies deeper, and goes to the heart of our economic system. This indeed was Charlotte Perkins Gilman's conviction; and her feminist Utopia is built on principles which derive from *socialism*.[12] Socialists come in many varieties, but all are united in the conviction that only thoroughgoing economic reform which establishes collective ownership of the "means of production" (a broad category including farmlands, factories, shops, processing plants, and so on) can ensure equality in society. The most substantive forms of inequality have their root causes and mechanisms of preservation in capitalist institutions: "free" enterprise, competition, the profit motive, exploitation of labor. As long as individual entrepreneurs roam freely through the economic landscape, annexing goods and property to themselves and allowing others access to them only at a cost, so long will systematic inequalities be ensured. For the profit motive ensures that each entrepreneur will prosper only to the extent that he extracts the maximum compensation from each person who wishes access to his goods, while giving the minimum compensation to those who labor in his service. The presence of other entrepreneurs in his neighborhood will exert some control over him, since he may lose his market and his laborers to a more favorable situation if he becomes too greedy. But the extent to which competition controls economic exploitation is debatable, in light of monopolies (a notable feature of U.S. economic life in the late nineteenth century), corporate mergers (a notable feature of

U.S. economic life in our own time), and other questionable facts of life in developed capitalism.

So socialists argue for massive economic reorganization, and *socialist feminists* believe that only thereby will gender equality be possible. Women and men experience economic disadvantage differently, and the differences are significant. For example, a disproportionate amount of women's work is uncompensated (domestic work and child care). Even those women who *are* employed as domestic laborers and child-care workers and who thus receive compensation (however meager), still face a high probability of an additional uncompensated "work-day" when they return home. [13]

In addition, capitalism provides incentives to keep labor costs as low as possible. Sexism ratifies additional reasons to rate women's labor contributions lower than those of men. Socialist feminists point to the earnings differential or wage gap between fully employed women and men in the United States today as presumptive evidence that this incentive to discriminate is being acted upon. [14]

But even more profoundly, socialist feminists lament the social and psychological consequences of living in a culture which rewards "beating out the competition," "killing off the other guy," and "coming out on top." A bumper sticker I occasionally see reads "The one who dies with the most toys wins," and the image this conjures up (a corpse surrounded by VCRs, Camcorders, and the like) often seems to me a sad testimony to the emptiness of the profit motive and the greed for competitive gain. Yet competition, profit, and gain are the heart and soul of a capitalist system.

Socialist feminists argue that the very concept of *community* is undermined by these aspects of capitalism; community requires shared concerns, a sense of cooperation rather than competition, and some sense of relatedness and collectivity. Thus Charlotte Perkins Gilman's socialist-feminist Utopia has citizens to whom both private property and individualist thinking are utterly foreign:

To them the country was a unit—it was theirs. They themselves were a unit, a conscious group; they thought in terms of the community. As such, their time-sense was not limited to the hopes and ambitions of an individual life. Therefore, they habitually considered and carried out plans for improvement which might cover centuries.[15]

And socialist feminists today offer powerful critiques of individualism in all domains of philosophy and of life, some of which we will have occasion to examine in subsequent chapters.

Although the precursors of feminist philosophy are numerous and diverse, this brief examination of Wollstonecraft's philosophical writings and Gilman's literary fiction acquaints us with two alternative political outlooks, the liberal and the socialist, through which a considerable amount of contemporary feminist thought can be glimpsed and understood. We move now to a look at the emergence of feminist philosophy within the Euro-American academic community: in the classroom, in the journals, in the lives of faculty and students.

ACADEMIC FEMINIST PHILOSOPHY

The *Philosopher's Index* gives a reliable overview of the interests and preoccupations of the Anglo-American philosophical community at any given time and across time. In 1969, the first year of its existence, the subject heading *Women* had one three-page article listed under it. (No subject heading for feminism or any related topic existed at that time. A random comparison is illuminating: In 1969 sixty-two articles on Wittgenstein were listed, and for three years the situation remained substantially unchanged. But in 1973 the subject heading *Feminism* appeared, with five articles listed.[16] The same year, under *Woman*, an article on Plato's philosopher-queens in the *Republic* was listed.[17]

The category of published philosophical work on feminism grew incrementally in the following two decades, until the 1989 *Philosopher's Index* contained 100 entries under *Feminism* (92 entries under *Wittgenstein*). What brought about this striking development, and what issues concern the authors of these philosophical articles and books?

Several historical factors seem to be major in fueling the earliest explicitly feminist philosophical projects: First, there had been, in response to the "second wave" of the women's movement in the United States and Canada, various legislative initiatives designed to encourage the hiring of women and minorities in areas of work in which they had been traditionally underrepresented. The women's movement itself was in part an outgrowth of the civil rights movements and the wave of student activism that accompanied escalation of the war in Vietnam.[18]

These legislative initiatives—such as Title IX, which ensured funding for women's athletics and others—had two immediate consequences for feminist philosophy: (1) They raised difficult moral and conceptual questions about the nature of equal opportunity, social justice, the moral status of affirmative action hiring programs, and the relationship between sex or gender and qualification for various types of work. Philosophers began to address these questions as they achieved pressing importance in the economic and political arenas. (2) The legislation ensured that women and minorities would at last have access to education, training, and finally employment in areas to which their entry had been denied in the recent past.

Thus the numbers of women in graduate programs within the academy, and in philosophy in particular (traditionally a male preserve) increased dramatically. In time, so did the number of women philosophy professors. While it should not be assumed that all women philosophy professors are interested in feminist philosophy or in so-called women's issues, it cannot be denied that women's presence in this academic discipline made a decisive difference in the nature of the pursuit of philosophy within the university and made feminist philosophy possible. Thus, from legislative change in the political arena feminist philosophy received two bursts of energy: one from the new set of topics that cried out for philosophical analysis and understanding, the other from the new set of philosophers, many of whom would be energetic in the pursuit of that understanding.

An additional factor influencing and encouraging the development of distinctively feminist philosophy comes from outside the academy; in fact, it hovers around the United States Supreme Court. Activists in the women's movement had for some years been especially interested in issues surrounding reproduction: the medicalization of childbirth, child care, access to birth control, and abortion. All of these areas are dense with moral and conceptual complexities and are overlaid in our society with webs of power and privilege, gender stereotypes, and authoritarian control. It might be said, in fact, that the way any culture treats reproduction in all its facets provides a concentrated glimpse into the conscience of that culture. During the 1960s, women in the United States were intensively examining that conscience and calling for change. In 1973, the Supreme Court of the United States issued its landmark decision in the *Roe* v. *Wade* case, overturning state statutes outlawing elective abortion. While the justices in their decisions and in their written opinions made appeals to the expertise of doctors, scientists, and theologians, they did not appeal to the expertise of philosophers, possibly because philosophers had been largely silent on the moral status of abortion. The decision, however, became the occasion for a vast philosophical literature not only on abortion but on all aspects of our reproductive and sexual identities as human beings and their social and legal ramifications.

From all of this it is clear that feminist philosophy owes its achievement of validity within the academy to events and processes that reach far beyond the ivy-covered walls. And feminist philosophers strive never to forget this debt; in fact, in their work, most of them remain grounded in social and political concerns, oriented to the problems of real and daily life, and connected to the realities of women's experience, and human experience generally, in all its deep particularities. In subsequent chapters we examine in more detail the ways in which traditional philosophy has largely resisted such involvement, and we look carefully at feminist critiques of the tradition along with detailed attempts to move beyond its limitations. But at this point it may be appropriate to sketch out some general features of feminist philosophy that can be traced back to the emergence of this way of thinking from concerns in the extra-academic world.

As we progress through our attempt to understand the engagement of feminism with traditional philosophy, we will see that there is a great deal of variation among feminist philosophers and that many schools of thought are thriving under their general banner. In fact, the majority of feminists both within and outside the discipline of philosophy are deeply committed to encouraging *pluralism* in all aspects of life. It is widely believed that there can be no more predictable way to go wrong than to insist that one's own views alone are right. The most straight-forward lesson to be learned about Western philosophy from a study of its history is that dogmatists quickly make themselves ridiculous. More significantly, the theories advanced by dogmatists seldom stand the test of even very limited time. Genuine philosophical understanding is best achieved through a collective process, in which the limitations of vision affecting one individual or group can be balanced by the differing visions of others. This insight is of the utmost importance to feminist philosophers and is the basis for a theoretical commitment to pluralism which allows us to regard disagreement as a source of inspiration and an occasion for growth. In what follows it must be understood that any generalizations about feminist philosophy are offered to simplify our access to its domain, not to give the impression that this thinking is monolithic or homogeneous.

SOME BASIC COMMITMENTS OF FEMINIST PHILOSOPHY

As women students and faculty (both minority and white) entered the academic world in ever-increasing numbers during the 1960s and 1970s, and particularly as they entered the philosophy classroom, many were quick to notice that traditional philosophy was (and to a noteworthy extent still is) a privileged white male project. From its legendary beginnings in ancient Greece, throughout its subsequent history, and up through the most recent national meetings of the American Philosophical Association, academic philosophy is dominated by an economic, racial, and sexual minority which has seldom hesitated to speak for the human race as a whole.

When this realization dawned on the minority and white women who were being drawn into the revitalized philosophical discourses surrounding social change, equal opportunity, reproductive control and freedom, and so forth, their reactions were diverse. Some felt that the domination of traditional philosophy by privileged white men was a temporary historical phenomenon, quickly passing and not likely to have made a large difference in the nature of philosophy itself. They argued that philosophy is a subject which, like mathematics or physics, has very little to do with the sex, race, or other particularities of the person pursuing it and much to do with the Nature of Reality. Truth is something that shows itself or hides itself equally with respect to all who seek it.

Others began to suspect that the problem might be deeper, its solution more difficult, than the mere passing of time and addition of women's voices to the debates could remedy. They began to look quite critically at the history of philosophy, keeping in the forefront of their reading the fact of philosophy's construction by a vocal minority and the specific nature of that minority along with its historical social position. Sometimes these critical readings provoked such frustration with the shortcomings of the texts under scrutiny that the students were driven to an outright rejection of philosophy. But at other times the results of this new way of reading philosophy's classical texts were intensely exciting. Instead of regarding, for example, Plato's dialogues as timeless products of the philosopher's quest for truth, we are now able to see them as issuing from a particular power position within an ancient culture's social system, as having historically specific polemical messages alongside their more general and potentially transcendent goals. In this way they come to life, take on a new humanity, and can be engaged with in more vital and personal ways.

Feminist philosophers now look not only at what is being said and by whom, but at who and what are being excluded from the domain of philosophical discourse, and for what reasons. Philosophers frequently make explicit or implicit restrictions on what counts as "real philosophy." A time-honored tradition extending back to the ancient Greeks, these restrictions work to delimit and define the class of potential philosophers. For example, the historical Socrates may well have maintained that real philosophers are to be found engaged in lively debate, lengthy conversations in which time limits should not be considered, in which the only meaningful thing is the pursuit of the truth. This directly suggests that those persons who cannot afford the time for such conversations, who have dependents needing care or duties which must be honored, cannot be philosophers. Socrates' material needs were taken care of elsewhere, and though he was not a wealthy man, his economic situation was such that he was not required to devote long hours each day to labors in the service of others. Of course, not everyone can do everything, but we need eggs to make an omelet and we need time to think philosophically. However, it is important to note that the very conception of philosophy constructed by Socrates, and by many of his intellectual heirs in subsequent centuries, makes it not only time-consuming but a *specialist's avocation*. Philosophical understanding will be the special possession of those, and only those, who can whole-heartedly and devotedly pursue it more or less full-time. The others will be the nonphilosophers, convenient for philosophers to have around when they are hungry or need new shoes, but not themselves party to the quest for truth.

This restrictive self-definition on the part of Western philosophy is a stunning development. For the very same philosophers who make of their studies a full-time pursuit and restrict access to their intellectual territory will also maintain the crucial importance of philosophical understanding to the fulfillment of human life. Thus wisdom, the *sophia* part of *philo-sophy*, will become a feature of the complete and even the morally good human being, in a way that clearly implies the defectiveness of the nonphilosophers.

This restrictiveness and elitism come in for sharp criticism from feminists. Philosophers are not to be allowed to have it both ways; *either* philosophical understanding is something only the few can possess after long and arduous mental labors, and is thus statistically similar to the ability to play Mah-Jongg extremely well, *or* it is a crucial element of human nature, a requirement for moral goodness and a complete life, and must therefore be potentially much more widespread in the human population (unless we are a dismally designed species). Feminist philosophers choose the second option, assume that human beings are adequately designed for the achievement of happiness and fulfillment, and attempt to construct interpretations of philosophical understanding which avoid the elitism and restrictiveness of past definitions. In doing this, they follow some general ground rules for philosophizing.

Rule 1: All our thought processes must be grounded in social and historical reality.

This means that the spurious generality of the philosopher's voice, in which he attempted to speak for all of humankind, must be resigned forever. The reality of human life is such that no one can truthfully and reliably speak for all of us; the desire to do so is arrogant in itself. Each of us brings to our thought projects a definite set of particularities: of race, economic class, gender, sexuality, early religious training, general political temperament and formal allegiances, societal and personal mores, and so forth. Not all of these are equally significant in their effects on all of our mental processes. Thus it may not be important for everyone to know that I was raised a Catholic when I give a public lecture on feminist art. But that religious training may well have a distinct shaping influence on my perception of certain forms of feminist art and certain specific artifacts. I cannot look at a nude woman doing performance art with large live snakes, for example, without being reminded of the Garden of Eden story, woman's status as "temptress" of man, certain lectures from nuns about "the girl's responsibility" to preserve not only her own virtue but her male companion's virtue as well, and more. Some of these memories may well deepen my appreciation of the performance art in question; some may merely distract me hopelessly from perceiving it for what it is.

This ground rule also means that the philosopher must be aware of the ways in which certain individuals or groups are implicitly *excluded* from the discourse. For example, in a class on the philosophy of sex and love, if all the hypothetical examples of relationships are heterosexual ones (as in the famous *Romeo and Juliet* example from Thomas Nagel's article on sexual perversion, which became a kind of paradigm for philosophical discussions of perversion and "normal" sex for some years[19]), then those persons who are not heterosexual are excluded from the philosophical universe. If in ethics classes the moral dilemmas considered are solely of the kind that arise in middle-class life, or moderately-to-amply privileged economic strata of society, then economically disadvantaged people are conveniently rendered invisible. If social and political philosophy are pursued from the standpoint of their Eurocentric tradition, then black and American Indian peoples will be ignored and thus intellectually erased from philosophy's scope. While it is not possible to think about and discuss more than a rather small number of things simultaneously, and therefore our philosophical discourse must of necessity restrict itself in numerous ways, it is not only possible but necessary to be cognizant of the nature of our self-restrictions, to remember who we are, what we are singling out for our contemplation, and what we are having to set aside temporarily.[20]

Rule 2: Take experience seriously, including the experience of feelings, emotions, and perceptions.

All of us are aware of the stereotypical image of the philosopher, who serenely ponders his puzzles or dilemmas with unruffled demeanor, with perhaps only a slightly furrowed brow to indicate that he is hard at work on something deeply profound. This fictional character has a long pedigree, tracking back in Western history at least to Socrates, and perhaps even before him to Anaxagoras. Concerning the latter it was said in antiquity that he philosophically consoled himself on hearing of the executions of his children by reflecting "I knew they were mortal when I fathered them".[21] The Socrates depicted in Plato's early dialogues, when faced with death, calmly debates our obligation to obey the law and explores the question of the soul's immortality, consistently remaining calmer than any of his conversation partners.[22]

The preternatural calm of the philosopher so described has its admirable features; it takes great courage to maintain one's equanimity in the face of tragedy and imminent death. However, the effect of this ideal on the concept of philosophical truth had its lamentable concomitants. Western philosophy has been marked by a distrust for the emotions, amounting at times almost to a pathological loathing for bodily experiences and perceptions, and for the passions which we experience and which define us as embodied creatures. This has left us with several problems, among which are a lack of philosophical understanding of the emotions in general, an incapacity for integrating emotional responses into our philosophical discourse, and a paradigm for knowledge which places the highest value on the most abstract, formal, non-physical representations of thought. As we will observe in detail in subsequent chapters, these problems have constituted a particularly pressing problematic area for feminist philosophers, since the tradition has defined women's nature in terms of the physical, the emotional, and the concrete. The moves of philosophers *away* from these attributes of human existence have entailed a corresponding distancing of women from the canonical philosophical domain. Traversing this distance has required both a critique of gender-polarizing conceptions of human experience and a reinvestment of philosophical topics and methods with the emotion, sensation, and passions they have so far too largely avoided.

The exclusion of women from the domain of the genuinely philosophical has perhaps, however, had the consequence *not* of totally squelching women's philosophical impulses but of forcing these to manifest themselves in unexpected ways, ways not recognized as orthodox within the dominant philosophy community. This possibility leads us to the next ground rule.

Rule 3: Look carefully for nontraditional sources of philosophical insight, for cultural artifacts created by those persons whose access to the orthodox institutionalized modes of philosophical expression such as published essays and books, lectures in halls of honor and learning, and so forth, has been denied.

The search for "the good, the true, and the beautiful" can be conducted in any number of ways, and with an unlimited array of materials. The prose essay may be a remarkably fine vehicle for the expression of certain sorts of understanding, but the poem, the vase-painting, the children's story, the novel, the conversation on the bus, the film, and the quilt may all be rich sources of insight as well. Feminist philosophers encourage us to ask the question "What *really* deepens my understanding of phenomenon X?" in a fresh and unfettered way, and not to be afraid of getting some answers which the stereotypical, placidly brooding philosopher might rule out.

Finally, the origins of feminist philosophy in real social struggle, both outside and inside the academy, are preserved in

Rule 4: Always bear in mind the social and political implications of your theories and other philosophical activities; these will be best and truest to the over-arching goals of feminism when they are geared toward social reform or liberatory change for all peoples. In a very real sense there is no such thing as an idle thought; all our thinking and all our behavior serve some set of purposes. Frequently we are unaware of these purposes, and sometimes our oblivion is relatively harmless. At other times, however, we are alarmed to learn of the practices we have been unwittingly supporting; we may think here of the cosmetics consumers who are horrified when they learn of the inhumane practices of animal testing which preceded the marketing of their favorite soaps and lotions. In much the same way, it is possible to wake up to the noxious effects of a philosophical theory, even one which is to all appearances quite well-intentioned. To give just one example: Marx's analysis of the exploitation workers suffer under capitalism was quite deliberately designed to be liberatory in its influence. Marx clearly felt the plight of the worker strongly, and had a deep conviction about the basic injustice of the relationship between propertied capitalist and propertyless worker. However, Marx seems not to have thought deeply enough about the differences between the statuses of men and women, or the ways in which their respective exploitations vary in an unjust capitalist system. He did not reckon domestic labor as labor, and therefore could not analyze it as exploitative or otherwise. Thus women's economic activities were obscured in his writings, and in subsequent Marxist and much socialist literature and practice as well.

So feminist philosophers attempt to keep in view at all times the ways in which their philosophical activities are affecting the world around them. Since the potential effects of any given action are in principle infinite and stretch far beyond the scope of any individual's awareness ("If I lift a finger, ocean ripples near Antarctica are affected"), this rule necessitates a lot of agonizing. Is it potentially liberatory to write monographs on Wittgenstein's philosophy of art? Only very remotely. But what if doing this allows me to keep my teaching job, in which I can encourage deepening social awareness in large numbers of students every year? Well, that sounds good. But what if keeping my teaching job *also* requires that I refrain from pointing out sexism and racism in the casual remarks of senior colleagues? Sounds like a shady compromise. And what if getting tenure requires that I avoid the time-consuming activities in the community that are more immediately productive of social change, like political campaigns, rallies, and working in a battered women's shelter? Facing these and other questions is part of the daily bread of feminist philosophy, and is actually just one particular way of striving to be a morally serious human being. While of course many philosophers have striven for moral seriousness, feminist philosophers are differentiated by the goal they seriously work for—human liberation—and by the methods they pursue—critique of the philosophical tradition and efforts to transform and vitalize it for an age of freedom, spiritual and physical health and safety, and human mutuality. It remains for the future to show whether such an age can be realistically hoped for; but it is certain that it will *never* come if human beings are unwilling to prepare for it philosophically. Feminist philosophy is attempting that preparation. Before we begin to examine just how, a word about philosophical *method* is in order.

"NOW GO FOR THE JUGULAR!"

While the stereotypical philosopher, launched on a wonder-project à la Aristotle's description, contemplates the phenomena on his mental field of vision serenely, certain philosophical practices have been at odds with the peacefulness of this picture. In my first year of graduate school, I experienced several different forms of culture shock while getting to know the domain of academic philosophy, but none was so severe as that experienced at my first departmental colloquium. All was well during the presentation of the paper itself, apart from the fact that it was enormously difficult to follow a monotone reading of a thirty-page technical treatise; but when the question-answer period commenced, all hell broke loose. I was shocked at the tenor of the questions; they seemed critical, negative, intending devastation of the speaker's argument. Some of those faculty who had not yet had a chance to attack waved their arms in the air frantically, moved restlessly in their chairs, and one muttered angrily under his breath. What had come over these decent civilized human beings whose souls had been refined by long association with "the life of the mind," "the realm of ideas"? I could only suppose that there had been some terrible flaw in the presentation, the argument was worthless; had I been able to follow it better, perhaps I would have seen it too. I felt pity for the speaker, whose career was surely at an end. Much to my surprise, at the end of the massacre, everyone jumped up happily; clapping each other on the back, shaking the speaker's hand, they all headed out for drinks and dinner.

Methods of discussion in academic philosophy have tended to be confrontational, at times quite aggressive. When I questioned my graduate adviser about the talk we had attended, he responded cheerfully: "You've got to develop your intellectual killer instinct. Go for the jugular!" The metaphors philosophers use, both in their written work and in conversation about what they do, tend to be combative; they "go a few rounds" with another philosopher, produce "knock-down" arguments, "go to the mats" (this one puzzled me for a long time, since I thought of prayer mats and meditation; actually it refers to wrestling). The language of attack and defense is routinely "deployed" (another cliché) to describe expressing and examining views. Feminist philosopher Janice Moulton has called this "the Adversary Paradigm" and has defined it as holding "that the only, or at any rate the best, way of evaluating work in philosophy is to subject it to the strongest or most extreme opposition."[23] The rationale is that, if one realizes all the while one is formulating an opinion that it will no sooner be expressed than others will be "moving in for the kill," one's views will be the strongest possible. No one will float idle opinions without being prepared to see them shot down. And in the process of giving full reign to their "intellectual killer instincts," the others are actually performing the valuable service of pruning one's thought projects back to their leanest and meanest, most defensible shape; for only the strong (ideas) survive.

There is clearly something of value in this confrontational process, apart from the fact that it has provided many an exciting conclusion to many a tedious colloquium. It is good to know that one will be challenged; it is healthy to have an atmosphere in which challenge is possible; and it is crucial to have as many ways as possible in which to learn about one's mistakes and oversights.

However, Moulton argues (and many feminist philosophers agree) that the "Adversarial Paradigm" has perhaps brought about more harm than good. It causes those who are participating in philosophical discussion to be cautious in their claims; a cautious thesis, a small thesis, a "programmatic" thesis (as in "This is only a suggestion and I haven't worked it out fully yet") do not always constitute either the best or the most interesting thesis. Confrontational rhetoric rewards the most agile and forceful arguer who is saying the least substantive thing possible. It also tends to focus the discussion on particulars within a project (via counterexamples and the like) rather than facilitating more wholesale discussion of conceptual frameworks. The latter enterprise, requiring as it does deliberation, care, lengthy and far-reaching statements, does not lend itself to the "cut and thrust" of adversarial debate.

Finally, in that the adversarial method awards the palm of victory in practice (not in theory) to the loudest voice and most forceful rhetoric, it tends to exclude women and others whose socialization or cultural values have not encouraged the development of such "killer instincts".[24]

Thus feminist philosophers call for and frequently employ alternative modes of discourse to the "challenge" mode. It is believed that confrontational models work to perpetuate exclusion, to keep silencing those who have been silenced in the past, to reward aggression (a predominantly masculine gender trait in Anglo-European culture). In addition, it is likely that the kind of philosophy which comes packaged in "knock-down" arguments is *not* the richest or most creative thought.

So, in addition to the above-noted substantive commitments of feminist philosophy I add this methodological commitment, which dictates that the "Adversarial Paradigm" be regarded with some skepticism, bearing in mind both its benefits and its costs when it is employed, and that it be supplemented with other conversational practices designed to encourage inclusion, facilitate dialogue, and sponsor creativity and a courageous philosophical imagination.

In subsequent chapters we explore feminist critical and constructive contributions to philosophy in several different areas, beginning with some of the most path-breaking and innovative movements in philosophy today: black feminist thought, American Indian feminist thought, lesbian philosophy, and environmental feminism—all areas not part of mainstream Western philosophy's purview, but ones in which rich alternatives to that tradition exist and are being further developed. We then study the ways in which aspects of traditional philosophy have been criticized; areas of specific focus include metaphysics, epistemology, and ethics. A final brief discussion surveys the main areas of agreement and disagreement within feminist philosophy today.

FOR FURTHER READING

Bartky, Sandra. "Philosophy and More Practical Pursuits: Philosophers and the Women's Movement," *International Journal of Applied Philosophy 4* (1989): 57–60.

Bartky, Sandra. "Toward a Phenomenology of Feminist Consciousness," *Social Theory and Practice 3* (1975): 425–439. Reprinted in *Beyond Domination: New Perspectives on Women and Philosophy*, ed. Carol C. Gould. Totowa, N.J.: Rowman & Allanheld, 1983.

Bordo, Susan. "Feminist Skepticism and the 'Maleness' of Philosophy," *Journal of Philosophy 85* (1988): 619–629.

Braidotti, Rosi. "The Subject in Feminism," *Hypatia 6* (1991): 155–172.

Code, Lorraine. "Simple Equality Is not Enough," *Australasian Journal of Philosophy*, supplementary volume 64 (1986): 48–65.

English, Jane. "Is Feminism Philosophy?," *Teaching Philosophy 3* (1986): 397–403.

Frye, Marilyn. *The Politics of Reality: Essays in Feminist Theory*. Trumansburg, N.Y.: Crossing Press, 1983.

Genova, Judith. *Power, Gender, Values*. Edmonton: Alberta Academic Press, 1987.

Gould, Carol. *Beyond Domination: New Perspectives on Women and Philosophy*; Totowa, N.J.: Rowman & Allanheld, 1984.

Gould, Carol. "The Woman Question: Philosophy of Liberation and the Liberation of Philosophy," *Philosophical Forum* (Boston) *5* (1973): 5–44.

Grimshaw, Jean. *Philosophy and Feminist Thinking*. Minneapolis: University of Minnesota Press, 1986.

Harding, Sandra, and Merrill B. Hintikka (eds.). *Discovering Reality: Feminist Perspectives on Epistemology, Metaphysics, Methodology, and Philosophy of Science*. Dordrecht: Reidel, 1983.

Harrison, Beverly W. *Our Right to Choose: Toward a New Ethic of Abortion*. Boston: Beacon Press, 1983.

Jaggar, Alison M. *Feminist Politics and Human Nature*. Totowa, N.J.: Rowman & Allanheld, 1983.

Lloyd, Genevieve. *The Man of Reason: "Male" and "Female" in Western Philosophy*. Minneapolis: University of Minnesota Press, 1984.

Lugones, Maria. "Playfulness, World-Travelling, and Loving Perception," *Hypatia 2* (1987): 3–19.

Nye, Andrea. *Feminist Theory and the Philosophies of Man*. London: Croom Helm, 1988.

Rose, Hilary. "Dreaming the Future," *Hypatia 3* (1987): 119–137.

Ruth, Sheila. "Methodocracy, Misogyny, and Bad Faith: Sexism in the Philosophical Establishment," *Metaphilosophy 10* (1979): 48–61.

Tong, Rosemarie. *Feminist Thought: A Comprehensive Introduction*. Boulder, Colo.: Westview Press, 1989.

Trimberger, Ellen Kay. "Women in the Old and New Left: The Evolution of a Politics of Personal Life," *Feminist Studies 5* (1979): 432–450.

Tuana, Nancy. *Woman and the History of Philosophy*. New York: Paragon House, 1992.

Vetterling-Braggin, Mary, Frederick A. Elliston, and Jane English (eds.). *Feminism and Philosophy*. Totowa, N.J.: Littlefield Adams & Co., 1977.

CHAPTER TWO

FEMINIST PHILOSOPHY IN NEW DIRECTIONS

The transformations feminist thinking has brought about in philosophy include not only new ways of working within traditionally established areas such as metaphysics, epistemology, and ethics (which we explore in subsequent chapters) but also the creation or recognition of new topics, areas of inquiry not previously considered part of an academic philosophy curriculum. In some cases, these areas are constituted by modes of thought which are part of ongoing traditions stretching far back in time, and feminists argue that their richness and integrity should be recognized and can function as a corrective to the narrowness of Western philosophy's traditional outlook. This is true of black feminist thought, American Indian feminist thought, and lesbian philosophies. In some cases, the philosophical problems are of recent origin, created by historical developments such as new art forms or technological advances, and they require new modes of thought to render them intelligible. This is true of feminist aesthetics, the ethics of reproductive technology, and environmental feminist philosophy. This chapter introduces several of these fresh and creative additions to philosophy's purview: black feminist thought, American Indian feminist thought, lesbian philosophies, and environmental feminism. Limitations of space both dictate this selectivity and limit the degree of depth in which each area can be explored. The goal is simply to introduce readers to the main issues in each of the three areas at the present time and thus to enable them to explore further, beyond the confines of this book. In addition, I hope to convey the sense of positive growth and transformation that are taking place in philosophy and invite the reader to take a personal part in the process. The old traditional boundaries of philosophy proper, like the walls of Jericho, have tumbled down; in feminist thinking, philosophy is not "theirs" but "ours," and it is ours to shape and direct as we see fit. The question "What can philosophy be *for you*?" is the question the reader needs to bear in mind throughout this book.

BLACK FEMINIST THOUGHT

We began this book with the reflection that the history of Western philosophy has been the particular purview of a relatively homogeneous group: privileged white males. A black perspective on the issues which philosophy's history brings under discussion has not been heard by the philosophical mainstream. If lack of privilege distances a group from participation in the knowledge-making institutions of a culture (as it clearly does), and if there are such things as skin privilege and gender privilege (as there surely are), it follows that black women have been particularly distanced from participation in the generation of knowledge, the activity of reflection, the doing of philosophy. For black women in Western history have experienced what some feminist scholars have called "triple jeopardy": they stand at the crossroads of cultural forces that privilege white skin, male gender, and economic advantage; they bear none of these privileges, and therefore they are denied three times.[1]

But to designate the situation of black women in white-dominated societies as one of triple jeopardy imparts two questionable assumptions: (1) The word *triple* leads one to suppose that the forms of disadvantage or oppression black women face are more or less present in all situations (and can thus be clearly counted); in fact, however, different social situations highlight different forms of privilege and therefore call for specific interpretations. In addition, (2) the "additive" model of oppression presupposes that gender privilege is experienced in the same way for all men, gender oppression in the same way by all women. This is to obscure the particular forms of privileging and oppression that are race-specific; a black woman is not situated in the same way within the gender-power system as is a white woman, nor is a black man positioned parallel to a white man. So some scholars call for a concept of "multiple jeopardy," which will allow us to look at specific social situations and understand the power configurations within them without presupposing that any individual feature has constant force (sometimes skin color is more meaningful than gender or economic class, sometimes less meaningful).[2]

In recent years black feminist thought has struggled with questions of priority of commitment; once we have developed an understanding of how power and privilege are related to gender, race, and class, what are we going to do about it? Is a commitment to a black liberation movement the logical place to start, leaving black women's issues aside temporarily? Or are there intense feminist priorities for black women which should not be put on hold?

Some black feminist thinkers maintain that, far from being either/or alternatives, the struggles for black and black women's visibility, respect, and fair entitlement to the goods of society are in fundamental harmony. They believe that the recovery of a powerful affirmation of black women's inherent spiritual strength and human worth will have liberatory potential for blacks in general. In this way they advocate a variety of black-feminist-standpoint theory, according to which the knowledge constructed from the specific epistemic standpoint of black women can cast a bright critical light on social forms in general, illuminating their logic in a particularly clear way and calling in a particularly clear voice for their rehabilitation.

We discuss feminist-standpoint epistemologies at length in Chapter Three. For present purposes, we can briefly define a "feminist-standpoint epistemology" as a theory of knowledge according to which the concrete realities of women's life situations, including daily work and relationships, constitute an outlook from which women may derive certain advantages (vis-à-vis men) as potential knowers. To give just one specific example, women in male-dominant cultures must learn to understand the thinking and feelings of the dominant men, while the men (because dominant) need not learn to empathize with women (though they may choose to do so out of interest, good-heartedness, curiosity, or for some other motive). Thus if a ready understanding of other human beings is of epistemic value, women's *standpoint* gives them a prima facie epistemic advantage.

One recent sustained and detailed attempt to provide a black feminist-standpoint philosophy is offered by Patricia Hill Collins in her book *Black Feminist Thought*.[3] Collins believes that we should approach the conceptual construction of such a standpoint with the awareness that black women's knowledge-making has been and largely remains a "subjugated knowledge" — a collection of forms of knowing not recognized as legitimate by the dominant or received-knowledge makers within the culture.[4] This means that we cannot simply look for the black woman's knowledge on the shelves of libraries or within the covers of journals; we must also go outside the traditional venues, to "music, literature, daily conversations, and everyday behavior".[5]

Collins finds certain core themes in black women's knowledge which ground the standpoint she describes. First, there is "a legacy of struggle," uniting black women in white societies down the generations and across economic boundaries.[6] From the days of slavery, through Reconstruction, up until the recent U.S. civil rights movement and the rapes, robberies, harassment, and beatings reported in the newspapers every day, black women have continued to struggle to survive and to create conditions in which their families can survive. This constitutes a shared legacy of strategies and strength. We can readily see that the work done by a person constitutes an undeniably important factor shaping that person's consciousness and thought processes. It would follow that the strength and courage black women have summoned in order to do their work of surviving in a culture in which, as Audre Lorde writes, "We were never meant to survive,"[7] along with the knowledge of the skills and strategies which they constructed for surviving, form a part of the black women's standpoint from which their thought will emerge.

A second core theme of black feminist thought emerges from critical analysis and deconstruction of what Collins calls "controlling images" of black womanhood, which have been promulgated through formal and informal knowledge channels flowing within the dominant white culture and have functioned to keep that culture from coming to understand black women, and to a lesser extent have also blocked self-understanding on their part. Collins discusses four such controlling images: the mammy, the matriarch, the welfare mother, and the jezebel (or whore). Mammies are cheerful providers of comforts in the homes or businesses of white people; they derive fulfillment from this service and thus are quintessentially subservient. Matriarchs head households because, due to their overbearing and domineering personalities, their husbands and lovers abandon them, necessitating that they become self-supporting by working outside the home. Since their children are supposedly then neglected, matriarchs are blamed for their children's academic failures and subsequent life problems. Collins shows this to be a widespread and classic example of victim-blaming.[8]

The welfare mother, an updated version of the breeder-woman image of slave ideology, is a matriarch without the energy to work outside the home. Her presence in the home has the same impact as the matriarch's absence, however; for she passes on bad values to her children. The controlling image of the welfare mother justifies practices designed to control the fertility of black women.[9] The jezebel is the sexually uncontrollable black woman whose aggressive sexual appetites are said to explain why she is the frequent victim of sexual assault. In Collins' view, the black-woman-as-whore image underlies all other controlling images and explains their logic; all devolve into ways of connecting "female sexuality, fertility, and Black women's roles in the political economy."[10] The only "positive" (i.e., approved by the dominant white culture) image is that of the mammy, who is usually depicted as "overweight, dark, and with characteristically African features—in brief, as an unsuitable sexual partner for white men."[11] Thus what is ruled out by these controlling images, taken together, is a black woman's control of her own sexuality.

By deconstructing these controlling images and replacing them with more accurate and positive self-definitions, black women participate in a social construction process in which they are active and creative—knowledge-makers rather than known (or misdescribed) objects. This activity and creativity are essential to the black feminist epistemological method pursued by Collins here and by other black feminist thinkers.[12]

The black women's standpoint also yields a different set of models for mothering than those prevalent in the dominant culture. Collins writes of the networks of women sharing child-care lore and work in black communities and of the practice of "othermothering," in which women take on some or all of the responsibility for children not their own biological offspring. Study of the actual conditions of life in African-American communities displaces the pernicious "controlling images" above discussed with a vision of "organized, resilient, women-centered networks of bloodmothers and othermothers" who cooperatively raise children, often with the active, hands-on help of male family members.[13] Attention to the dynamics of these communities would perhaps provide some helpful guidance in nonblack communities as well. Some important psychological theories about child development embraced by many feminists, such as the "object-relations" theory (to which we return in Chapters Three and Four), are built on a family model which is starkly different from this one, and which raises problems which do not arise for the black family as Collins describes it. Specifically, it has been argued that the solitary female caregiver and absent-at-work male-head-of-household nuclear family cause gender-differentiated maturation patterns for males and females and give rise to identity problems for both sexes. Both the lines of maturation and the identity formation would be different for the black child in the more collaborative household.

A specifically black feminist epistemology will have, Collins argues, four components:

1. It will adhere to concrete experience as a criterion of meaning, making personal knowledge and subjective wisdom the arbiters of epistemic significance.

2. It will employ *dialogue* as a method of validating knowledge claims.

3. The black feminist epistemology will also incorporate an ethic of caring, in which an emphasis on the uniqueness of each individual (an emphasis traced by Collins to a long-standing tradition of African humanism) leads to valuing individual expression—the voice and point

of view, the heart-wisdom, of each person will be considered a cherished contribution to the collective knowledge-making.[14] Other elements of this caring ethic will be an emphasis on the appropriateness of emotion in cognitive pursuits, or a resistance to the rationality/emotion dichotomy (which, as we see in subsequent chapters, is an important theme for many other feminist philosophers), and a focus on *empathy* as a condition for dialogue and human connection.

Though Collins introduces many examples from African-American experience and culture to substantiate this caring ethic, she offers a single one that covers all three aspects: the call-and-response discourse found in black religious services. In this interactive form of worship, preacher and congregation *together* create a fervent religious dialogue in which rhythm, tone of voice, and cognitive content meld inextricably to create the meaning of the service. Collins writes:

The sound of what is being said is just as important as the words themselves in what is, in a sense, a dialogue of reason and emotion. As a result it is nearly impossible to filter out the strictly linguistic-cognitive abstract meaning from the sociocultural psychoemotive meaning.[15]

4. Finally, the black feminist epistemology will incorporate an ethic of personal accountability, in which makers of knowledge claims will expect to be held accountable for their knowledge claims, to be willing to argue for them and to exemplify their coherence with the claimer's basic ethical commitments. This is similar to Lorraine Code's conception of epistemic responsibility, according to which knowers must be constantly alive to the ethical ramifications of their claims, at the personal and the social levels.[16]

In summary, then, black feminist philosophy contains an emphasis on creative reconstruction, according to which the new values and lifegiving ideas, which will displace the oppressive and outworn frameworks of our privilege-ridden present and past, are consciously crafted out of a dialectical engagement with the minority traditions of the past. For Collins' version of black feminist thought it is stipulated that these values and ideas are built out of a thorough knowledge of how the tradition has worked against black women (focusing on the control of their sexuality), and of efforts to reclaim longstanding African and African-American traditions whose value cannot be seen from the perspective of the dominant philosophical ideals of white Anglo Western culture. Here, as elsewhere in feminist philosophy, caring is placed at the center of the value scheme and along with accountability forms an epistemic as well as a moral requirement. And the role of emotion in thought and action is to be reassessed and given greater determining significance.

This philosophical outlook promises to have liberating ramifications for black people generally, and thus to transcend the dichotomous rhetoric of "identity politics" ("black or feminist?"), because it is squarely based in realities of black experience that have been suppressed or ignored by the dominant culture, and because it provides an empowering standpoint from which to value those realities and argue for the social changes needed to promote and maximize their free and undistorted future flourishing. In other words, black feminist philosophy can provide the conceptual groundwork for a general black social liberation movement and process.

AMERICAN INDIAN FEMINIST THOUGHT

In the enormously popular 1990 American film *Dances with Wolves,* the Sioux people at one point are shown deliberating about how they should react to the lone white soldier who has taken up residence in the abandoned camp nearby. A gathering, consisting entirely of men, sits in a circle inside a tent; all who wish to speak are allowed to do so, and the film writer's evident intent is to illustrate the democratic nature of Indian political processes. When the men decide to adjourn without having made a definite decision, the viewers may well admire the care, thoroughness, and open-endedness of Indian politics. As they leave, the viewer is shown where the women of the village have been during this meeting: They are gathered all about the door and bottom edges of the tent, their ears pressed to the walls, desperately attempting to overhear what is being said.

In this film, Kevin Costner set out with all good will to depict Plains Indian culture in a nonprejudiced way, a way that would acknowledge the beauty and value of traditional Indian ways and get past the lamentable Hollywood stereotypes of Indian people and their lives. He stumbled badly with this scene, however, and over an issue that has befuddled white men since they first began to encounter Indian life: the centrality of Indian women to the political life of their societies. Though one should not make generalizations about "Indian society" as if it were homogeneous, there is undeniably a strong tradition of gynocracy (rule or governance by women), matriliny (inheritance of tribe, clan, and band membership along a female line), and of institutions valuing women's thoughts and practices, woven throughout many tribes' cultural histories. Paula Gunn Allen writes:

Even among Plains people, long considered the most male-oriented Indians, at least by the media and its precursors in popular culture, power was and is gained, accrued, mediated, and dispensed only through the grace and beneficence of female influence.[17]

Many white women and men are profoundly surprised upon learning of the roles and powers accorded women in Indian cultures, so thoroughly have they been mystified and suppressed by Anglo-European thinking. The media image of the squaw as a passive, timid, hard-working, and heavily burdened second-class citizen is both widespread and false.

Like black feminist philosophy, Indian feminist thought also must be sought out not only on the shelves of libraries and within the covers of standard academic journals but also in the novels, poetry, and social activism of Indian feminists. Thus Paula Gunn Allen, an important source for this chapter and elsewhere in this book, develops her feminist theory from study of the poetry of Joy Harjo, Mary Tallmountain, and others, the novels of Leslie Marmon Silko and others, along with careful readings of Indian history and of the traditional stories and rituals which have been so vital a part of Indian life.[18] Also like black feminist thought, Indian feminism begins from the acknowledgment of a long history of brutal oppression, and the knowledge that in spite of that oppression, "Indians endure."[19] In the case of the Indian people, the history they have endured in this country since the arrival of Europeans has been one deliberately designed to annihilate their culture altogether. Indian feminists argue that a recovery of the traditional woman-centered ways of life and thought will be a powerful force for strengthening Indian identity and culture.

Indian feminist thought is thus quite different from that of many schools within the Anglo-European feminist community; the latter begin from a perception of women's oppression or subordination and study a centuries-old tradition in which gender privilege, skin privilege, and social power are accorded to wealthy white men, denied to women. Indian feminists by contrast look back on centuries of gynocentric culture, interrupted in relatively recent historical time by the arrival of bearers of that very culture which Anglo-European feminists are denouncing.[20] Thus while the Anglo-European feminist is sometimes at a loss to describe in any great detail the social system she envisions as liberatory, Indian feminists can point to specific social forms of their past, and formerly vital philosophical beliefs, as concrete starting points.

Among these philosophical foundation-beliefs of traditional Indian life, two are of particular relevance to themes of this book: (1) *the centrality of women,* and of female principles, in structuring human experience and preserving the relationships with the sacred or spiritual elements of the universe; (2) *the interrelatedness of all of the natural world,* not in the contingent sense that "everything's beside something else" but in the profound sense that nature constitutes a living and sensitive system in which there is neither randomness nor loss. I will discuss these separately.

(1) Maria Chona, a Papago Indian woman whose life story was published under the title *Papago Woman* in 1936, was an "executive woman" or leader in her band. She says this about women's nature:

You see, we *have* power. Men have to dream to get power from the spirits and they think of everything they can—song and speeches and marching around, hoping that the spirits will notice them and give them some power. But we *have* power.[21]

Chona's firm assertion of power reflects the widespread assumption within Indian cultures of the value and strength of women. This assumption is grounded in part by Indian spirituality, in which feminine spirits frequently are credited with both the creation and the maintenance of the universe, along with provision of the conditions allowing human life to continue.

Writing of such feminine spirit divinities as White Buffalo Woman, Thought Woman, and Corn Mother among the Lakota Sioux, Paula Gunn Allen points out that they have both a sustaining and a connecting power within human life:

Without the presence of [Corn Mother's] power, no ceremony can produce the power it is designed to create or release. These uses of the feminine testify that primary power—the power to make and to relate—belongs to the preponderantly feminine powers of the universe.[22]

For contrast, we can think of the dominant religions of the Judeo-Christian tradition, in which a supposedly genderless but somehow quite masculine deity ("God the Father" in Christian teaching and prayer) both creates and sustains the universe. Primary power in these religions is exercised by a masculinelike being who involves women in His providential plans only as deputies or clerical workers. (Recall Mary's response to the proposal that she give birth to God's Son: "Behold the handmaid of the Lord! Be it done unto me according to Thy Word!"—a response of total submissiveness.)

Western culture has most frequently interpreted power as "power over," and the very term brings to many people's minds images of clenched fists, arms raised over another person's cowering body, flexed biceps, readiness to exert force. For this reason some feminist thinkers have been skeptical even about the popular word *empowerment* as naming an acceptable feminist goal; do we want *power* of this kind? Indian feminists point out that the sense of the term which derives from their tradition is not in this way hierarchical or violent; it connotes rather the strength of the bonds connecting people in community, a connection which is renewed in ritual and ceremony and realized in the shared life of the band and the extended family. It is a power in solidarity, rather than in opposition and domination. It thus provides a very illuminating alternative conception to that which the mainstream Western culture has constructed.

(2) The interrelatedness of all aspects of nature, and of human life within the texture of nature as a whole, is also a core belief of Indian

philosophy. A recurrent theme in the poetry of Joy Harjo is the idea of a conversation between humans and various aspects of nature; the "speech" of nature, of lakes, clouds, the earth and sky, can be heeded or ignored, but is unceasing. For example, in her poem "For Alva Benson, and for All Those Who Have Learned to Speak," Harjo describes the earth as speaking and being heard at the moment of a child's birth:

And the ground spoke when she was born.
Her mother heard it. In Navajo she answered. . .[23]

As the child grows up and learns both English and Navajo, she travels to cities populated by people "learning not to hear the ground as it spun around / Beneath them. . .," learning to be oblivious to the earth's speech. Yet ". . . the ground spinning beneath us / Goes on talking." The vision of nature as intelligent and communicative is one expression of the Indian belief that humans and nature are akin, that the natural world is a benevolent order in which all things are related and are in themselves worthy of respect.

Allen writes:

We are the land. To the best of my understanding, that is the fundamental idea that permeates American Indian life; the land [Mother] and the people [mothers] are the same. . . . The earth is not a mere source of survival, distant from the creatures it nurtures and from the spirit that breathes in us, nor is it to be considered an inert resource on which we draw in order to keep our ideological self functioning. . . . Rather . . . the earth *is* being, as all creatures are also being: aware, palpable, intelligent, alive.[24]

Thus human life and the life of nature are not just interrelated in the sense that we depend on nature for food and other "raw materials," and we have effects (sometimes disastrous) on nature when we procure those raw materials. Rather, nature's life and ours are a complex unity, the balance and beauty of which must be respected as a condition for the survival and continuation of all its constituent elements. (We pursue this as a very promising basis for an environmental feminist philosophy in the next section.)

In Chapter One we viewed the distanced and abstracted model of "the philosopher" who contemplates or "wonders" at the phenomena of human existence from a safe and privileged distance. We saw also that, when this philosopher descends into dialogue with other thinkers, he or she frequently enters with "gloves off" and "goes for the jugular" when opposed. We saw also that certain individualistic aspects of the ideal liberal-democratic citizen and state make genuine shared human community problematic. Some of traditional Western philosophy's central problems, and some central problems for Western culture as well, proceed from a distancing of the self from other selves, fracturing of communities into hostile or marginalized segments, elevating an epistemic elite above the heads of the workaday world. Even the brief glimpse into traditional Indian philosophies we have just taken is sufficient to show that Indian thought does not give rise to these problems. Starting from a conception of the self in relation, and of the system of physical nature as inclusive of humans and as intrinsically intelligent and worthy of respect, and positing women's power and worth from the outset, both step around many traditional Western philosophical problems and give a firm foundation for feminist philosophy. Thus Indian feminist thought calls for the careful examination, and ultimately the revitalizing and reclaiming, of a system of thought and social life which have been pushed near extinction.

LESBIAN PHILOSOPHIES

Among the groups conspicuous by their absence from the purview and concerns of traditional philosophy, lesbians are prominent. Gay men can look to the glorification of male-to-male passion in Plato's works for at least some evidence of their existence as a subject in Western philosophy; nonlesbian women are (to their peril) philosophized about too on occasion; but lesbian existence is totally ignored in the classics of Western thought.[25] Philosophy is not alone in this erasure, for lesbian invisibility is a feature of Western culture and its artifacts quite generally up until the most recent years.

Nor has even fairly recent feminist writing entirely resisted the powerful societal impulse to proceed as if lesbians were virtually nonexistent. Kate Millett's *Sexual Politics,* for example, is a true landmark work in American feminism in which the underlying political messages of erotic literature in English are carefully analyzed. It has proven enormously influential and has sparked an entire new school of literary criticism, sensitive to the sexual dynamics of literary texts in ways unheard of prior to Millett's work. Yet even in this work, which was first published in 1969, lesbians appear only in the following surprising way:

Following custom, the term "homosexual" refers to male homosexual here. "Lesbianism" would appear to be so little a threat at the moment that it is hardly ever mentioned [in pornography]. . . . Whatever its potentiality in sexual politics, female homosexuality is currently so dead an issue that while male homosexuality gains a grudging tolerance, in women the event is observed in scorn or in silence.[26]

Admittedly, Millett's focus is on pornographic literature, but the social comment about "female homosexuality" being a dead issue is striking—and representative of the general cloak of invisibility with which lesbians have been obscured.

One of the central aims of feminist thinking in its contemporary renascence has been to "create space" for lesbian existence. There are several reasons why this is a general feminist aim rather than simply a lesbian project. First, the oppression lesbians have experienced has been far more intense than women's subordination generally; it has involved violence, disenfranchisement, ostracism, and danger that go beyond "mere" sexism. These actions show that lesbian existence is a powerful challenge to male-dominated culture, for we attempt to destroy only that which threatens us deeply. Secondly, lesbians are women who have separated themselves from the central values of patriarchal culture to some degree or other, which gives their thinking a valuable critical distance from the essential engines of that culture. It is in the interests of all feminists that this thinking be encouraged to flower. Finally, feminists are committed to the belief that, to the extent that one group is oppressed, all are reduced in humanity; thus there is a general devotion to the elimination of oppression which is by now a familiar theme to us.

Lesbian philosophies are those thought projects in which lesbians strive to reshape or re-create the fundamental categories of philosophical thinking in such a way as to render them affirmative of, rather than destructive to, their own most cherished values. The plural ending of *philosophies* is of great importance, for reasons that will emerge shortly.

But, given that lesbians have now been acknowledged to exist, one might ask, why is there a need for new philosophies or new philosophical methods just for lesbians? Does a person's sexuality dictate the shape of that person's philosophical understanding? This is a legitimate question, and there are several different ways to go about answering it.

First, not all lesbian philosophers do maintain that philosophy needs to be remade from the ground up in order for them to feel comfortable within it. They express concern about "reinventing the wheel," a phrase encapsulating a common feminist concern about becoming too critical of traditions, too quick to reject what might after all be valuable and even necessary.[27]

Second, however, it is useful to think about the extent to which institutions that affirm heterosexuality as *the* norm for human beings dominate our cultural landscape. If we are heterosexuals, we can fail to notice these; they are present as an affirming background for all our experience, so constant that they become virtually undetectable, like the hum of fluorescent light fixtures. For example, there is the widespread societal assumption that everyone we see and meet is heterosexual. For heterosexual people, this is a very relaxing assumption to make; we know these roles: girlfriend, guyfriend, married, available, someone-I-can-flirt-with, someone uninteresting. All these roles take shape in a landscape of heterosexuality. What happens if someone we've been assuming to be heterosexual reveals herself/himself or is revealed as lesbian or gay? Now what roles will there be for us? I once had occasion to observe how upsetting this can be and to observe it from an interesting perspective: that of the person formerly assumed to be heterosexual, now assumed to be a lesbian. I was on a search committee for the hiring of a university administrator, and one of the interview questions I chose was this one: "How would you as an administrator plan to foster growth for the diverse constituencies of our university community, such as lesbian and gay people?" One candidate of whom I asked this question stands out in my memory for his extraordinary body response: His face changed completely in an instant; he stared at me in what can only be called shock, his eyes actually narrowed and hardened somehow, and I realized, "He's reinterpreting me as lesbian." His response to the question itself was almost inarticulate, and someone else mercifully jumped in with the next issue. But as we left the room, he and I reached the door at the same time, and he stood back with both hands raised, to let me pass without threat of contact. I'm almost certain that this was involuntary.

This extraordinarily interesting and revealing experience was for me only a momentary glimpse into the kind of reaction lesbian and gay people must deal with daily. It showed me vividly that, for this person, I was a comfortable human being *only* as long as I was taken to be heterosexual.

The philosophical significance of this assumption of heterosexuality, and the diffusion of this assumption over the landscape of daily life, is that we may plausibly suppose that Western philosophy, like the astonished job candidate, is not well set up to accommodate lesbian concerns. It is for this reason that many feminists believe a new starting point and new methods for philosophizing are called for.

Though the issues being discussed in lesbian philosophy are quite numerous and the approaches being taken quite diverse, I focus here on just one area in which lively and constructive debate is occurring; we may call this area lesbian epistemology. (Chapter Four discusses feminist epistemologies in general, but I introduce lesbian epistemology here because its quite specific origins in lesbian experience make it unique and deserving of separate treatment.)

A strong theme running through much lesbian feminist thought about knowledge, how it is acquired, and how it is diffused throughout communities of knowers is the importance of *personal epistemic responsibility* or *authenticity*. It is of vital importance, it is argued, for individual lesbians to take up the project of generating their knowledge claims out of their own experience and from their own standpoints. Since heterosexuality is so pervasive, and has proved itself so inhospitable to those who decline to follow its behavior directives, the conceptual frameworks, the categories of understanding, the theories of knowledge and justification which lesbian philosophers have been taught are all to some degree or another antithetical to their own authentic ways of thinking. In other words, lesbians have been taught thought patterns that speak against the validity of their very existences even as thoughts are uttered. This emphasizes the urgency of recovering the genuine, the vital, and the true from beneath the distorting superstructure that has been imposed upon it. This also underlines the enormous difficulty of the task, a difficulty to which we will shortly return.

A second strong, closely related theme concerns the *avoidance of epistemic imperialism*. I use the term *epistemic imperialism* to denote the making and promulgating of knowledge claims that illegitimately include others within their scope; for example, the claim "We all know that men are insensitive" illegitimately attributes to all in the group being addressed a view that may well be the speaker's alone (and may also be false). Joyce Trebilcot has argued for the central importance in her own lesbian philosophy of adhering to the principle "I speak only for myself." She also writes eloquently of the enormous difficulty of adhering to this principle in practice.

. . . I say that I speak only for myself. The truth is, however, that often I speak also for men. The self who speaks is contaminated by patriarchy and so—I hate this—sometimes I am like a computer, a parrot, a talking box, putting out the stuff men have put into me: classism, racism, ableism, disdain for the earth, more. That I intend to speak only for myself does not mean that I speak always in accordance with my chosen values.[28]

We can already see that lesbian epistemology will be more radically *pluralistic* than most of the standard theories of knowledge which have gained currency in the Western tradition. Traditional philosophy has not for the most part been agile at accommodating the simultaneous occurrence of competing or diverging views. Lesbian epistemologies are at work generating frameworks within which decisive differences of beliefs and convictions can exist without generating the felt need to rule one or more of them incorrect. In doing so they must avoid absolute relativism, according to which (for example) "All lesbians should be exterminated" would be valid. How might this work?

To answer, we must remind ourselves that theories of knowledge do not appear apart from certain specific ethical or valuational commitments which both motivate them and ground their meaning within the larger pattern of human activities. Lesbian epistemology as we have been describing it takes its initial motivation from the commitment to recovering and developing a philosophical voice that has been silenced in the past and is thus shaped by an adherence to the principle of nonsuppression, nonsilencing. The hypothetical person who would claim equal time for the utterance of extermination calls is operating out of a valuational network exactly opposite to this principle of nonsuppression. He or she cannot coherently claim the protection of the pluralism inherent in lesbian epistemologies for the intrinsically nonpluralistic, difference-*negating* prescription uttered.

Some lesbian philosophers call not only for new epistemic principles but for new *forms* in which to develop these principles. Thus Jeffner Allen frequently chooses the form of poetry over the traditional philosophical essay or colloquium presentation as more liberatory and enhancing of the imagination. She explains this choice as a deliberate rejection of the drastic separation of philosophy and politics from poetry accomplished in part by Plato, who in the *Republic* argued that poetry must be banished from the ideal state because of its emotional potency.[29] Allen advocates the use of just this emotional potency to invigorate philosophical discourse and empower the creative imagination.

Marilyn Frye has written of the need for an epistemic *attitude* different from that in which all phenomena of human experience are interpreted in relation to the needs and desires of a male epistemic elite.[30] This limiting interpretive stance she labels "the arrogant eye"; it well encapsulates the epistemic imperialism we noted above as opposed to lesbian epistemologies' starting points. To counter the lingering effects of the "arrogant eye" on our own thinking, Frye proposes an epistemic attitude she calls "the loving eye," one in which women are affirmed, women's projects and values are affirmed *in their own right*, without reference to their utility for patriarchal projects. Achieving this stance is, Frye acknowledges, a difficult task requiring a courageous imagination, the kind of imagination Jeffner Allen's choice of the poetic medium is designed to enhance. Frye writes:

There probably is really no distinction, in the end, between imagination and courage. We can't imagine what we can't face, and we can't face what we can't imagine. To break out of the structures of the arrogant eye we have to dare to rely on ourselves to make meaning and we have to imagine ourselves beings capable of that: capable of weaving the web of meaning which will hold us in some kind of intelligibility. . . . We need to know women as independent: subjectively in our own beings, and in our appreciations of others. . . . The loving eye does not prohibit a woman's experiencing the world directly, does not force her to experience it by way of the interested interpretations of the seer in whose visual field she moves.[31]

Thus Frye's challenge is that we learn to know without *arrogating*, without appropriating the known to ourselves and forcing it to assume the contours we are expecting; that our epistemic stance be one of affirming, not of assimilating the independent existence, reality, and value of the known.

In Chapter Five we return to lesbian philosophy, to examine lesbian ethics; elsewhere in that chapter we further develop the theme of *love* in relation to perception.

To sum up lesbian epistemologies, though, we have seen them adhering to the following principles: (1) Personal epistemic responsibility or authenticity is the starting point for knowledge projects; (2) Epistemic imperialism, of the sort that has pervaded so much of Western philosophy, is to be studiously avoided; (3) An ethically bounded pluralism is to be embraced, one in which different views are not competitors but mutually enriching possibilities; (4) Innovative forms for philosophizing may be sought and encouraged; and (5) An epistemic attitude of affirmation of the independence of the known, a "loving eye," is to be sought. We see some of these principles affirmed in the next section.

ECOLOGICAL FEMINIST THOUGHT

An essay by Alice Walker entitled "Am I Blue?" tells of the way in which a brief friendship with a horse changed the author's life forever. The horse, named Blue, lived in a field next to the land on which Walker and her companion rented a house for three years. She got into the habit of feeding him apples from a nearby tree which he couldn't reach. Startled to be reminded how expressive horses' eyes were, she was "unprepared for the expression" in Blue's eyes. It told her that "Blue was lonely. Blue was horribly lonely and bored".[32] As a child she had known that animals can express themselves, can "communicate quite well;" but adulthood brings forgetfulness of this.

Walker meditates on other contexts in which the expressions of others are ignored or mystified; she thinks of the white people raised by black "mammies" who somehow forget, when they've passed a certain age, that their caregivers were fully communicative and intelligent human beings. She thinks about the Asian women who marry white men, and of how happy these marriages are during the period when the wives speak little or no English: "What then did the men see, when they looked into the eyes of the women they married, before they could speak English? Apparently only their own reflections." And she speaks of the way each generation forgets what it felt like to be a teenager, and reacts to young people's behavior with impatient incomprehension.

In Walker's essay, Blue is eventually given a companion, and for some months he is blissfully happy. During this time,

[T]here was a different look in his eyes. A look of independence, of self-possession, of inalienable *horse*ness. His friend eventually became pregnant. For months and months there was, it seemed to me, a mutual feeling between me and the horses of justice, of peace. I fed apples to them both. The look in Blue's eyes was one of unabashed "this is *it*ness".

But one day the companion is taken away. The misery in Blue's eyes then is almost unbearable to behold:

It was a look so piercing, so full of grief, a look so *human*, I almost laughed (I felt too sad to cry) to think there are people who do not know that animals suffer. People like me who have forgotten, and daily forget, all that animals try to tell us.

"Everything you do to us will happen to you; we are your teachers, as you are ours. We are one lesson", is essentially it, I think.

What Alice Walker's essay conveys is one of the central tenets of feminist environmental philosophy: that the human capacity to distance ourselves, to separate and to alienate ourselves, that important precondition for all forms of exploitation, is *paradigmatically* expressed in our attitudes toward nature and animals. Insofar as we can distance ourselves from animals, we can justify treating them as mere means to our human ends. Insofar as we can distance ourselves from nature, resist being regarded as part of a larger order in which humans and the nonhuman realm are reciprocally interrelated, we can get excited about changing nature all around—dominating it, "harnessing" it, even creating new forms of it. This model of humans' relation to the rest of the natural world, "man" the distanced manipulator and controller, lends itself readily to the intoxication with technology in which Western culture finds its head reeling today. This intoxication, along with the view that nature is that domain which lies ready at hand for prediction, control, and exploitation, have produced the worldwide ecological crisis which depresses us so at the present moment in history.

Ecological feminist philosophers point out that attitudes toward *women* and toward *nature* exhibit an uncanny resemblance; this is not surprising in view of the fact that the central controlling ideologies of our Western tradition define both in terms of their "otherness," their "difference" from the (male) human norm which stands at the center and defines.[33] The reader may recall from Chapter One Edmund Burke's comment that "A woman is but an animal, and an animal not of the highest order." Such popular slang expressions for women as "fox," "bitch," "vixen," "kitten," and others accord with Burke's sentiment.[34]

Thus, it is argued, the political causes of women and of ecology are conceptually linked. A clear analysis of the culture's attitudes toward *both* promises to provide a solid basis for critique and transformation.

Environmental philosophy itself, whether of feminist or nonfeminist emphasis, is a relatively recent development. While some provegetarian philosophers such as Daniel Dombrowski trace vegetarian arguments based on animal rights as far back as Porphyry (Second century A.D.), the development of a literature and an activism based on concern for preserving species, maintaining ecosystems, and minimizing animal exploitation and torture is a response to abuses in all these areas, the recognition of which is a recent phenomenon.

Feminist environmental philosophers are critical of many nonfeminist contributions in this area, arguing that they tend to remain within the very conceptual systems which justify the abusive practices in the first place. Thus, they argue, a feminist critique is needed in order to move us beyond the old distancing, dualizing, and domination-justifying thought patterns.

The animal rights literature is a case in point. Val Plumwood has argued that nonfeminist animal rights advocates tend to get trapped in certain dualisms which undermine the force of their arguments.[35]

For example, she criticizes the Kantian framework within which Paul Taylor's book *Respect for Nature* is developed. Taylor maintains that the attitude of *respect* for the inherent worth of a person or thing is the only morally respectable and defensible ground for treating it well; inclination and emotion are not relevant to morality. Plumwood writes:

Respect for nature on this account becomes an essentially *cognitive* matter (that of a person believing something to have "inherent worth" and then acting from an understanding of ethical principles as universal).[36]

But this way of dichotomizing reason and emotion is bound up with the privileging of the mental, the intellectual, the "truly human" over the natural and the physical; and *these* privileges are at the root of most mistreatments of animals and the destruction of ecosystems, the very problems environmental philosophy sets out to solve!

In some cases, environmental philosophers betray the androcentric and human-valorizing attitudes in a slightly different way, by grafting onto the natural world concepts which apply properly only to human society. This is essentially a failure to acknowledge the diversity of the planet, the real and unique integrity of the nonhuman world. For example, Tom Regan's 1986 book *The Case for Animal Rights* sets out to argue for animal rights based on a conception of rights drawn from

John Stuart Mill according to which "if a being has a right to something not only should he or she (or it) have that thing, but others are obliged to intervene to secure it".[37] The vocabulary of rights, however, is designed for individuals with potentially competing interests in human political and legal contexts. Its application to nature at large, and especially to "predators in a natural ecosystem," leads to all kinds of absurd results. We would be morally obligated to "intervene massively in all sorts of far-reaching and conflicting ways to secure the rights of a bewildering variety of beings" if rights were accorded even only to the higher species.[38]

Mainstream animal rights arguments have tended to apply the liberal model of the self, as composed of a bundle of interests which it wishes to have satisfied, to nonhuman animals.[39] This approach, which Deborah Slicer links to essentialism (defining an entity on the basis of a single trait or capacity) has led to some absurdities. Peter Singer concludes his well-known article "Animal Liberation" with a bizarre question:

What, for instance, are we to do about genuine conflicts of interest like rats biting slum children? I am not sure of the answer, but the essential point is that we *do* see this as a conflict of interests, that we recognize that rats have interests too. Then we may begin to think about other ways of resolving the conflict—perhaps by leaving out rat baits that sterilize the rats instead of killing them.[40]

This passage is surely one of the most peculiar in the history of Western philosophy! First, is it significant that the example of "interest conflict" involves slum children (rather than scions of European royal families)? Perhaps not, but it is just possible that the even-sidedness of the interest conflict which Singer is urging is less outrageous when slum children, whose interests may not seem so compelling to us, are balanced opposite rats. Note also Singer's helplessness at resolving the conflict; his only proposed strategy is a "techno-fix" that would tell us nothing about the ethics of an immediate situation of rat bite. It would in fact probably endanger the slum children still further, because of the introduction of a strange new chemical substance into their living environment. What happens to toddlers who eat rat-sterilizing baits? But again: How is Singer's proposal even morally justifiable, on his own

grounds? Don't the rats have interests in rat sexuality too? In rat reproduction? Within Singer's utilitarian framework, would not an equally
justifiable proposed solution be the sterilization of slum *mothers?* But
the weirdest aspect of the passage is Singer's apparent emotional distance from the hypothetical situation he describes; as if *anyone* would
stand idly by, balancing "competing claims," while a child was
gnawed by a rat! That the overwhelmingly probable human response
does not even occur to Singer to mention here is telling. Something has
gone badly wrong in the theory kitchen to cook up this befuddled
result.

Mary Midgeley has suggested that a more promising basis for com-
prehending the ethical ramifications of animal-human interactions is
the concept of *feelings* rather than interests, rights, or intellectual
capacities. For, as we saw through our brief examination of Alice
Walker's essay at the beginning of this section, the fact that some animals experience and express feelings seems to many people undeni-
able. Pain brings a clear response from many kinds of animals, as does
pleasure. But feelings more akin to genuine emotional states also
appear to be experienced by animals, and this fact is a basic premise of
most pet-owners' attitudes toward their pets. Perhaps we should start
from this consideration, and avoid the bracketing of emotion as a stable
grounding moral characteristic that is our legacy from Descartes and
Kant.

Some feminist environmental philosophies also urge that we develop
a *caring* attitude toward nature that would extend beyond animals to
inanimate things such as mountains and rivers. This is to appeal to the
vocabulary of an ethic of care (discussed further in Chapter Five) and
apply it outside the human domain. Karen Warren has written that a
meaningful experience of a natural environment calls forth an attitude
of attentive love similar to that described by care-based ethics.

Others have argued that this is problematically vague; we are sometimes at a loss as to what the caring response is in human situations, so
how much more confused would we be when trying to formulate the
caring response to streams and rockfaces? Others have expressed concern that this kind of thinking would anthropomorphize the natural
world in ways feminist philosophers have counseled us to avoid.

Deborah Slicer makes a call for moral integrity in our dealings with the environment, which is in some ways reminiscent of the call for accountability made by black feminist Patricia Hill Collins. Slicer urges that we think hard about the tension between our permissiveness toward cruel treatment of laboratory animals and our exaggerated sentimentality toward our pets (pet cemetaries, expensive surgeries to prolong life, beds and special luxury foods, and so on). She also suggests that those who eat meat should visit slaughterhouses and meat-packing establishments, to make sure they know experientially what is the previous history of their hamburgers.[41] This is not to prejudge our responses to this knowledge, only to stress that we should not avoid the full comprehension of the meaning of our practices.

In conclusion, then, feminist ecological philosophy calls for a move beyond the alienated unemotional self, the abstract context devoid of natural human response, the tendency to project human political concepts onto the realm of nature, thereby denying its uniqueness and integrity, and avoiding what Karen Warren has called "logics of domination."[42]

To say all of this is not to say that there will suddenly emerge simple answers to the enormously complex ecological problems which face us. But feminist philosophers urge that we keep in mind the effects of these beliefs on women and other "others" which mainstream Western philosophy has either created, supported, or condoned. If it has worked to marginalize women, to mystify their lives and concerns, to ratify oppressive social orders, then it will probably *not* work as the basis for an environmental philosophy that can bring us nearer to a harmonious relationship with nonhuman nature.

This concludes our brief survey of some of the new directions feminist philosophy is taking today, in areas not covered by the canon of traditional Western thought. In the following chapters, we turn to an examination of the ways in which feminist philosophers are critically interrogating that canon and developing ways in which the traditional topics and concerns of philosophers can be revitalized from a feminist perspective.

FOR FURTHER READING

Allen, Jeffner. *Lesbian Philosophy: Explorations*. Palo Alto, Calif.: Institute of Lesbian Studies, 1986.

Allen, Paula Gunn. *"Hwame, Koshkalaka*, and the Rest: Lesbians in American Indian Cultures;" *The Sacred Hoop: Recovering the Feminine in American Indian Traditions*. Boston: Beacon Press, 1986. Pp. 245–261.

Brant, Beth. *A Gathering of Spirit: A Collection by North American Indian Women*. Ithaca, N.Y.: Firebrand, 1984.

Brown, Wilmette. *Roots: Black Ghetto Ecology*. London: Housewives in Dialogue, 1986.

Cheney, Jim. "Ecofeminism and Deep Ecology;" *Environmental Ethics 9* (1987): 115–145.

Daly, Mary. *Gyn/Ecology: The Meta-Ethics of Radical Feminism*. Boston: Beacon Press, 1978.

Davis, Angela. *Women, Race, and Class*. New York: Vintage, 1983.

Dill, Bonnie Thornton. "Race, Class, and Gender: Prospects for an All-Inclusive Sisterhood," *Feminist Studies 9* (1983): 131–150.

Griffin, Susan. *Woman and Nature: The Roaring Inside Her*. New York: Harper & Row, 1978.

hooks, bell. *Ain't I a Woman? Black Women and Feminism*. Boston: South End Press, 1981.

hooks, bell. *Talking Back*. Boston: South End Press, 1989.

King, Ynestra. "Feminism and the Revolt of Nature;" *Heresies* 13:Feminism & Ecology *4* (1): 12–16.

Lorde, Audre. *Sister Outsider*. Trumansburg, N.Y.: Crossing, 1984.

Lorde, Audre. *A Burst of Light*. Ithaca, N.Y.: Firebrand, 1988.

Moraga, Cherrie, and Gloria Anzaldua (eds.). *This Bridge Called My Back: Writings by Radical Women of Color*. Watertown, Mass.: Persephone Press, 1981.

Narayan, Uma. "Working Together Across Difference: Some Considerations on Emotions and Political Practice;" *Hypatia 3* (1988): 31–47.

Merchant, Carolyn. *The Death of Nature*. San Francisco: Harper & Row, 1980.

Mohanty, Chandra Talpade, Ann Russo, and Lourdes Torres (eds.). *Third World Women and the Politics of Feminism*. Bloomington: Indiana University Press, 1991.

Palmer, Phyllis Marynick. "White Women/Black Women: The Dualism of Identity and Experience in the United States;" *Feminist Studies 9* (1983): 151–170.

Plant, Judith. *Healing the Wounds: The Promise of Ecofeminism*. Santa Cruz, Calif.: New Society Publishers, 1989.

Plumwood, Val. "Ecofeminism: An Overview of Positions and Arguments;" *Australasian Journal of Philosophy* supplementary volume 64 (1986):120–138.

Rich, Adrienne. "Compulsory Heterosexuality and Lesbian Existence," *Women, Sex, and Sexuality*, ed. Catherine R. Stimpson and Ethiel Spector Person. Chicago: University of Chicago Press, 1980.

Spelman, Elizabeth V. *Inessential Woman: Problems of Exclusion in Feminist Thought*. Boston: Beacon Press, 1988.

Warren, Karen J. "The Power and the Promise of Ecological Feminism," *Environmental Ethics 12* (1990): 125–146.

Warren, Karen J. (guest ed.) Special issue of *Hypatia: Journal of Feminist Philosophy* on ecological feminism. 6(1) (1991).

Williams, Patricia. "On Being an Object of Property;" *Signs 14* (1989): 5–24.

CHAPTER THREE

BODY, MIND, AND GENDER

We have already had occasion to observe that much of Western philosophy has displayed a definite discomfort with the fact that human minds come in human *bodies*, that consciousness and the thought processes it underlies are embodied in more or less gross matter. It is not very difficult to understand some of the motivations behind this discomfort. For thoughts do not seem to be subject to the same limitations as ordinary physical objects; in imagination, I can accomplish things which seem to transcend the limits of space and time. Vivid memories defy the irrecoverability of the past, seeming to bring to life dead friends, bringing into the present past scenes, meals, and dreams. Dreams themselves are a powerful impetus toward regarding the mind as something more than or different from the physical "container" which it "inhabits" (though we shall soon see reasons to question these terms). And personal identity, the "I" who is the location of my consciousness, stretches back in time to embrace the child I was, the adolescent I became, and the woman I am now, even though in the physical sense I can only claim to be exactly what I now am (the past being no longer present).

Thus there are certain prima facie reasons for at least questioning how consciousness, thought, dreams, and identity relate to the physical world. But we will see that quite often philosophers have gone much further than questioning the relationship, to the extent of privileging the mental over the physical, derogating the physical and the human body along with it to a secondary ontological status, counseling efforts to transcend the body in order to apprehend truth, and even regarding the fact that mental events can cause physical events as a miracle performed by God on a daily basis! While this last, far from being a majority view, seems to have been instead a desperate expedient recommended only by one philosopher (Malebranche), it is symptomatic of something having gone badly wrong at the philosophical starting point.

Let us look more closely at the way in which the relation between body and mind, and the status of the body in the grand scheme of things, become problematic for philosophy. As our companion in this inquiry we will choose René Descartes—whose philosophical outlook, especially as represented in the designedly popular work *Meditations on First Philosophy* (published in 1641), proved enormously influential and remains a standard component of introductory studies of Western philosophy today.

SOLITARY MEDITATIONS, RADICAL DOUBTS

Descartes' work came at an extremely crucial juncture for Western philosophy. He entered a philosophical milieu still largely dominated by the medieval scholastic tradition, itself based heavily on a theologized and incomplete digestion of the legacy of the ancient Greeks. Studying with the Jesuits at the college of La Flèche, he received a "classical" and rather intellectually conservative education. Descartes made a radical break with this tradition, however, and set institutional philosophy off in a wholly new direction. Seeking to provide a philosophical method which would be accessible to all who possess common sense, providing a set of "rules for the direction of the mind" which would be so simple that "even women" would be able to follow them, his contributions to philosophy were revolutionary and of inestimable worth and influence.[1] His contribution to the topic of this chapter, however, is highly problematic; and the difficulties he bequeathed to subsequent modern Western thought are enormous.

The full title of Descartes' *Meditations* is *Meditations on First Philosophy: In Which the Existence of God and the Distinction Between Mind and Body Are Demonstrated*.[2] This full title is instructive as to how Descartes himself viewed his purpose in the work, which is often read in

modern terms as a refutation of skepticism or an essay in foundational-
ism. By his own description, it is a work of *metaphysics*.[3]

Descartes begins by confessing that he has long been aware that false
beliefs have formed a part of his world view, and that a general and
total mental "housecleaning" would need to be undertaken, in order to
discover which of his views should be retained and which discarded.
The procedure for this belief-testing, which he now proposes to under-
take (since he is at present free "from every care" and "happily agi-
tated by no passions")[4] is that of *doubting*. He will attempt to cast
doubt on each of his present beliefs; only those that survive the doubt
ordeal will be retained. Rather than holding up individual beliefs for
scrutiny, however, he proposes to address their general bases:

. . . [I]t will not be requisite that I should examine each [belief] in particular,
which would be an endless undertaking; for owing to the fact that the destruction
of the foundations of necessity brings with it the downfall of the rest of the edifice,
I shall only in the first place attack those principles upon which all my former
opinions rested.[5]

This project raises several interesting issues. First, Descartes is firmly
committed to a *hierarchical* view of the structure of his belief system.
The metaphor of the edifice of opinion, an ordered structure in which
there is a top-down organization of architectural form, is an epistemological image to which we return in the next chapter when we discuss
images of belief systems, and the power of the metaphors we choose to
represent cognition.

But note also the extreme *solitude* of Descartes' project here. He is
proposing to take apart and rebuild his entire belief structure in isolation from the rest of the world, and particularly from other human
beings. The idea that an epistemological value test could reliably be
applied in complete isolation from other knowers, that one's own relations of knowing the world could be tested through demolition and then
rebuilt to stringent specifications entirely of one's own devising, is
extraordinary.[6] When we consider the contexts in which knowing takes
place, in which knowledge is sought and constructed, few of these
appear to be ones in which isolation is afforded or even desirable (we
might think of archeological digs, science labs, classrooms, reading

groups, research institutes, fact-finding missions to other countries, courtrooms, and other typical situations in which knowledge is found and formed in human minds; none is an individual-based project).

Thus Descartes is setting himself an *artificial* kind of task, in the dual sense that his knowledge-seeking environment is atypical and that the envisioned "new and improved" cognitive structure or edifice of opinion will be his *own* individual artifact.

But the solitariness of Descartes' project has also another implication/motivation. Only in radical isolation from the rest of the human social world can Descartes *fully* explore the reliability of his entire belief system. For if he were exploring in collaboration with others, if the meditations he undertakes were the work of a Cartesian task force, he would have to make concessions to the reliability of certain beliefs before the task force could begin its work. He would have to trust that the others were thinkers, perhaps even thinkers on a par with himself; that they were working with him rather than against him, that they could have and work toward a common goal, that their words could be understood, trusted, believed, taken more or less at face value. In other words, the Cartesian project could not motivate total doubt if it were not so solitary. The powerful skeptical doubts which Descartes is about to summon into existence will answer only to the call of an isolated individual human mental voice. They are creatures of solitude. Descartes' individualistic starting point has lasting and dramatic effects on his total project and its overall outcomes.[7]

THE UNCERTAIN BODY

As the doubt program progresses, Descartes discards his trust in his senses as a source of reliable belief. Since (he reasons) the senses have deceived him in the past, it is advisable to suspend belief in sensory information for the duration of his meditations until he can uncover some justification for their occasional reliable operations.

But the senses have been the source of his belief that he is an embodied creature, that he exists in or as a physical organism, in addition to being an originator of thoughts. Thus he must suspend his belief in the existence of the embodied Descartes and conceive of himself only as a locus of thoughts and other mental events, possibly not embodied at all, possibly embodied very differently from the way he has always pictured and experienced himself:

> I shall . . . suppose, not that God who is supremely good and the fountain of truth, but some evil genius not less powerful than deceitful, has employed his whole energies in deceiving me; I shall consider that the heavens, the earth, colors, figures, sound, and all the other external things are nought but the illusions and dreams of which this genius has availed himself in order to lay traps for my credulity; I shall consider myself as having no hands, no eyes, no flesh, no blood, nor any senses, yet falsely believing myself to possess all these things; I shall remain obstinately attached to this idea. . . .[8]

Descartes will conceive of "himself" as something independent of his body, and he will discover in this incorporeal consciousness the one indubitable truth which will function for him as an Archimedean immovable point, from which his belief structure can be rebuilt. This point is the certain truth of his own existence.

Descartes has effectively divided himself, and his belief structure, into two components: the certain mind, the component in which he will repose confidence at least as to its existence, and the uncertain body, about whose reality he will remain in a state of doubt until complex argumentation proves a limited trustworthiness, a constricted and carefully policed reliability.

Armed with the certainty of his own existence (as an insular node of consciousness which may or may not be embodied), Descartes goes on to demonstrate the existence of God, the fact that God is neither a grand deceiver nor the kind of being who would tolerate such massive deception of his creatures, and finally infers that the senses' urgings toward belief are not in themselves so awfully unreliable after all.

But the body, on Descartes' showing, remains forever only a probability, never a certainty. Since certainty is the Cartesian Holy Grail, this means that the body is irredeemably a second-class citizen in the metaphysical scheme of things. First rank in Descartes' universe is held by "thinking things," nodes of consciousness that can through purely rational processes follow deductive argumentation to absolutely certain conclusions. The body cannot participate in this process with its own humble abilities, here conceived as sensation and perception; it either impedes the rational process or, tamed and disciplined, stands dumbly by and lets knowledge happen.[9] Highest epistemological honors go to the elements of deductive reasoning processes: mathematical laws, logical principles, indubitable truths. These construct the knowable core of the world, and to them in human experience is superadded a "flesh" of more dubious nature: bodies, colors, touches, smells, and the entire organic contents of the universe.

This theme, the privileging of the mental over the physical, does not originate with Descartes by any means. It is familiar to readers of Plato, who describes the relationship of soul to body in vivid terms:

> . . . [W]hen the soul uses the instrumentality of the body for any inquiry, whether through sight or hearing or any other sense—because using the body implies using the senses—it is drawn away by the body into the realm of the variable, and loses its way and becomes confused and dizzy, as though it were fuddled, through contact with things of a similar nature. . . . But when it investigates by itself, it passes into the realm of the pure and everlasting and immortal and changeless. . . . [Phaedo 79c–d][10]

Here the body is cast in the role of a bad companion, bad company for the soul to keep, company that drags it down to its own level and impedes its effective functioning. A nonphysical form of knowing, in which the soul or mind operates "by itself," is much to be preferred.

Two features of this way of discussing the relation of mind to body, common to Plato and Descartes, should be noted. First, it is striking how easily both drop into the mode of thought in which a human being becomes not one but two, and two *different*, kinds of entity. There quickly emerges a kind of logical and metaphysical distance between mind and body, an alienation that provokes disagreement about what to believe, what to seek, how to behave. But secondly, this is not a disagreement among equals. The mind or soul is in Descartes' view the locus of certainty and value, in Plato's view the part of the human composite akin to the "pure" and "divine." Its relationship to the body is to be one of dominance; the body is to be subordinated and ruled.

An individual human being contains within the self, therefore, a fundamental power dialectic in which mind must triumph over body and must trumpet its victory in flourishes of "pure" rationality by means of which its soundness is demonstrated and ratified. Far from being an isolated peculiarity of a small handful of philosophers, moreover, this general dialectic is seen being set up and played out in many theaters of Western culture, from religion to popular morality, from Neoplatonism to existentialism.

THE UNCERTAIN OTHER

A recent and particularly interesting manifestation of Descartes' legacy to subsequent philosophy was the so-called problem of other minds that obsessed certain Anglo-American philosophers during the first half of the twentieth century and still interests some today. The problem is set up by questions of the form "How do I know that there are other minds?" "How do I know that the supposed person to whom I'm now speaking really has a mind, instead of a bunch of computer hardware and a clever program?" "How do I know that my mind is not the *only mind in the universe?*"

Introducing this problem to people who are not already convinced of its importance is a curious experience. Polite students and nonacademic philosophers often seem to be stifling a temptation to laugh, and some people find the questions personally insulting ("Who are you calling robot?!"). Nevertheless the problem of other minds has painfully exercised many academic philosophers and generated many a symposium, seminar, and collection of essays. Much of the literature devoted to the problem is decidedly strange in tone. For example, a 1938 article by H. H. Price delivers this eerie description:

Suppose I hear a foreign body utter the noises, "Look! there is the bus." I understand these noises. That is to say, they have for me a *symbolic* character, and on hearing them I find myself entertaining a certain proposition, or if you like entertaining a certain thought. . . . I now proceed to look round; and sure enough there is the bus, which I had not seen before and perhaps was not expecting yet. This simple occurrence, of hearing an utterance, understanding it, and then verifying it for oneself, provides some evidence that the foreign body which uttered the noises is animated by a mind like one's own.[11]

If experiences of this kind recur "in connection with this particular foreign body," if (continues Price) "I am often in its neighborhood" and "it repeatedly produces utterances which I can understand" and verify, then

I think that my evidence for believing that this body is animated by a mind like my own would then become very strong. It is true that it will never amount to demonstration. But in the sphere of matters of fact it is a mistake to expect demonstration. . . . If I have no direct extrospective acquaintance with other minds, the most that can be demanded is adequate *evidence* for their existence.[12]

The evidence will be most compelling when "the utterance I hear gives me new information; that is to say, where it symbolizes something which I do *not* already believe. For if I did already believe it at the time of hearing, I cannot exclude the possibility that it was my own believing which caused the foreign body to utter it."[13]

In other words, strong evidence for the foreign body's mentality would not have been provided by its making noises about something platitudinous, such as the weather. A comment like "Nice day isn't it?" will cut no ice with the careful philosopher of mind, who demands to be brought some new and surprising epistemological treasure by the foreigner craving acknowledgement.

What really happens at Price's bus stop, and what is its significance for Cartesian dualism, mentalism, and the metaphysics of body and mind? A "foreign body" (which, Price specifies, need not be human, but may be an animal or a gorse bush) makes "noises" that allow Price to "entertain a certain proposition," initially neither believing nor disbelieving it. Fortunately for the foreign body, a bus does indeed materialize, Price sees it and thus verifies the noises as true and sensible speech. This does not quite suffice for the conclusion that the foreign body probably has a mind, however; to prove this the foreign body must virtually follow Price around, making appropriate, comprehensible, and verifiable noises "in many different kinds of situations." At some point during its exhausting labors, it will be awarded the accolade of "other mind" by the satisfied Price. He will have good evidence for supposing that "this body is animated by a mind like my own." At last then, its foreignness overcome or redeemed, this other mind can rest on its record of good linguistic and mental behavior and be welcomed to the mind club.

Now, Price may well be having some (presumably) innocent fun with his foreign bodies and noises, but the configuration of this putatively social situation deserves comment. Price does not concern himself with demonstrating that he himself has a mind, in order to persuade the foreign body that he is mentally competent or kin to *it*; rather he subjects the other to the evidential test. Price, like the Cartesian ego, carries about within himself the standards by which the others are to be judged; he peers out from an inner fishbowl of certainty onto a world which must prove itself to *him*. This proof must be delivered in terms he can understand, and tested by criteria which he can employ and which he establishes as valid. It is but a small step to view Price (or the philosopher of mind he is representing here) as a kind of colonialist in the domain of the potentially mental; the "foreign body" must learn his language and is admitted to the fraternity of minds by demonstrating its similarity to the colonist, adopting his manners, telling its humble but sometimes novel truths to him over and over again "in many different kinds of situations" until it gains acceptance.

It is not an insignificant detail that the foreign body must make its noises in the King's English, on the strict terms of Price's example. If it addressed him in a language unknown to Price, then Price would be unable to "entertain a certain proposition" in response to it, and all the more unable to "verify" the state of affairs the noises describe.

And there is a solitary silence inside Price's mental world. The noises the foreigner makes cause mental events inside the fishbowl, but their causation is via symbolism; it is as if the foreigner held up placards for Price to contemplate, and the cogency of the message on the placards determines Price's inner response ("mind like mine" or "something alien"). Their exchange cannot be described as a communication until the informational content of the noises is assessed. Yet clearly the informational content must be communicated before it can be assessed.

The problem of other minds is situated within a highly specific conceptual terrain, one in which the isolated human subject is afloat in a sea of uncertainty, plagued by indecision about his or her most attractive inference patterns, left to go it alone with only the dimensions of its own fishbowl within which to trust. Yet this ego has definite power, for it imposes its self-generated standards on the field of its experience, demanding that that field prove itself or be consigned to what Descartes called "darkness." Beginning from a point in secure isolation, the Cartesian–Pricean ego is unable to reconnect itself with the universe "outside" the body it "animates"; neither can it successfully connect with that body itself. Yet its isolation has a certain imperial splendor: Lone though it be, the insular ego feels comfortable in, perhaps even morally obligated toward, demanding that the world meet *its* standards. It is much like the unhappy tourists in a foreign country who insist in a tone of unmistakable moral indignation that their favorite homeland breakfast be served.

What, if anything, is wrong with this picture? We saw at the beginning of this chapter that there is considerable intuitive force behind philosophy's disposition to distrust the body; and Descartes' distinction between the certainty of his consciousness and the uncertainty of its physical embodiment has a certain cogency.

Additionally, science fiction has lent vivid presence to the fear that others might not in fact be like us mentally. An episode of the television series *The Twilight Zone* presented an astronaut spaceship-wrecked on a distant planet who is overjoyed to be joined by a mysterious but beautiful woman. She becomes his lover; they work arduously to rebuild his broken ship. She displays an uncanny ability with complex machinery. When the longed-for day of departure arrives, she refuses to accompany him. Furious, he grabs at her hair and succeeds only in ripping off her face—behind which complex circuitry, rather than flesh, is revealed. He then leaves her willingly after a bitter diatribe: "You're just a machine!" Yet he had loved her. And she might have passed Price's tests with flying colors. So perhaps modern life may present us with the problem of other minds at bus stops after all.

But feminist criticism of mind–body dualism, and of the privileging of the mental, has been wide-ranging and intense.

FEMINIST CRITIQUES

We have already noted the extraordinary isolation of Descartes' metaphysical musings; he cuts off not only the instructions of his perceptive faculties, but also the entirety of his human social surroundings, to seek a certainty accessible only to the lone and insular conscious node "I." A feminist critique of Cartesian method might well begin with just this feature of his project.

The Cartesian ego, rather than being the ground for certainty and the Archimedean point which some philosophers have taken it to be, may in fact be the result of a mistaken abstraction. Feminist philosophers such as Caroline Whitbeck and Lorraine Code have convincingly argued that a preferable starting point for understanding the contents of human consciousness is *the relational self*, the self presented as involved in and importantly constituted by its connectedness to others.[14] Each of us at this moment is connected as it were by invisible threads to an indefinite number of specific other human beings. In some cases, these connections are relatively remote; for example, we are all members of the same species and have biological similarities. Similarity is a relationship; therefore we are all related. Western culture has not tended to place much weight on this species relationship, however, and in some notorious institutions such as chattel slavery the reality of the relationship has been implicitly or explicitly denied. In other cases, the relationships in which we now stand are of deep significance in defining who we are, how we think, and how we act.

Starting with the concept of the relational self would greatly have changed the course of Descartes' meditations. If other persons are not just colorful wallpaper the design of which I contemplate from inside a mental fishbowl but actually part of who I am, then distancing myself from them in thought and supposing that I am the only consciousness in the universe becomes, if not impossible, extremely illogical. What would I hope to accomplish? If on the other hand I begin by granting them mentality and humanity, I will proceed by considering the specific ways in which their contributions to my mental life are made.

Paula Gunn Allen writes that, in Native American cultures, the question "Who is your mother?" is another and more profound way of asking who one is. In asking, one is inquiring about one of the most significant parts of a person's identity, for the influence of the mother and the mother's contribution to the child's self is considerable.[15] In much the same way, we might begin a metaphysics of the self by asking "To whom am I related? In what ways? What contributions to my consciousness are presently being made, and by whom?" Such a beginning acknowledges the fundamental importance of sociality in human existence.

Here it might be objected that Descartes' and H. H. Price's methodological skepticism about the existence and reality of other minds remains a possible position even for a relational self. Haven't we merely sidestepped the skeptical possibility by granting the mentality and humanity of the others? Doesn't it really still seem possible that they are all phantasms, or robots, or results of direct C-fiber stimulation by a mad scientist on a distant planet?

Yes, skeptical possibilities remain and cannot be ruled out. But taking the standpoint of the relational self allows us to affirm that such possibilities *do not matter.* What matters is that relationships are granted metaphysical priority over isolated individuals, so that the embeddedness of the self in a social world becomes its primary reality. The exact nature of the individuals involved becomes a matter of secondary importance. I grant at the outset that others make constitutive contributions to my experience, and I to theirs. This mutual interrelation becomes the ground for any further inquiry rather than functioning as a more or less uncertain inductive conclusion. Thus, to return to the problem of other minds, we can see that the philosopher's uncertainty about the mentality of the "foreign body" at the bus stop is a symptom of a flawed starting point rather than a genuine puzzle attending our reflective lives. The philosopher's mistake is to begin from isolation and attempt to reason himself back into society; we in fact begin in society and this is not an accidental but a deep truth about us.[16]

We might go even further and argue that the concept of a radically isolated subject as the seat of consciousness is simply incoherent. We do not begin to think and speak in solitude, but in concert with our culture and with the specific representatives of the culture in whose care we find ourselves. We form ourselves in a collective process that is ongoing; our thoughts are never entirely our own. Intersubjectivity is basic, while individual subjectivity is secondary and an abstraction.

Some feminist philosophers have analyzed the isolation of the ego and the "fishbowl" syndrome of some philosophy of mind in terms of differences between masculine and feminine gender socialization. Developmental psychologists have suggested that the structure and dynamics of relationships with other human beings differ profoundly for traditionally socialized men and women. Due largely to the fact that, in most cultures and historical epochs, women function as the primary caregivers for children of both sexes while men enter into the life of the family in a more intermittent way, it is to be expected that male children will form their earliest sense of themselves by *distinguishing* themselves from their female caregiver, realizing that they are members of the group from which the (distant, absent, or intermittently present) male family members derive. Female children will form their sense of themselves by *identifying* with the female caregiver, realizing that they share with her membership in the group of female family members.[17]

This early direction of the sense of self, either to distinguish oneself and differ from, or to identify oneself and resemble, leaves a lasting legacy in the child's heart and mind. The adult character which emerges from the socialization process is marked by the tendency toward either clear and stark ego boundaries (if male) or flexible and mobile ego boundaries (if female). A whole constellation of dispositions and traits goes alongside this basic distinction. The masculine ego, formed at a distance from its primary role exemplar, displays a lifelong tendency toward independence, distancing from others, and endless acts of "proving" the masculinity which it modeled, with some uncertainty, on the distant fellow *man*. The feminine ego, formed in close proximity to its primary role exemplar, has lifelong tendencies toward identifying with others, reciprocating feelings, being dependent on others and relating to them easily, even confusing its own needs with those of others—since it early on perceived that part of being a woman was to place others first, as a primary caregiver must frequently do.

This developmental thesis about gender identity, though impossible to demonstrate empirically and almost certainly *not* valid crossculturally or crossracially, offers a tempting explanation for the philosophical model of the isolated self we have traced in Descartes and seen lurking behind the problem of other minds. The Cartesian ego is quintessentially *masculine* in its solitary doubting program, in its self-confidence about its quest, in its ambition ("proving" itself all on its own resources), and in its uneasiness. And H. H. Price's philosopher at the bus stop is a perfect product of masculine identity development; he demands that the other prove itself by his standards of mentality, he initially conceives of himself as cut off from the other and hears the language of the other as "noises," and he alienates and is alienated. He begins with suspension of assent to the alien's propositions, and only when he *sees the bus for himself* does he believe ("I'll expect it when I see it!").

By contrast, the relational self which some feminist philosophers have proposed as an alternative starting point for philosophy of mind, and for grounding our understanding of human experience generally, is more aligned with feminine identity development.

In addition to proposing that philosophers start from a conception of the human self as relational, as situated within a web of cultural and personal relationships which not only shape but do much to constitute its being and its thought, feminist philosophers have also criticized the Cartesian legacy for the relation between mind and body which it conveys.

We saw above that Descartes (and others) operate from a position that separates mind, self, consciousness, ego from the physical body these are said to "inhabit" or, in H. H. Price's term, "animate." In Descartes, the distinction is so drastic that mind and body are said to share no attributes whatsoever; they are oppositionally defined and thus, metaphysically speaking, mutually exclusive. Consciousness is nonphysical, nonextended, and inhabits an order of being completely distinct from that in which the body lives. The body is a machine, operated by the mind in the case of the human being, mindless and purely mechanical in the case of other animals.

This drastic dualism is vulnerable to criticism from many different directions; feminist critics begin with the observation that in Western

culture and throughout its history, we can observe a tendency to identify women with the natural, the physical, the bodily. Nature is person-
ified as a female, a "mother"; women are portrayed as more closely
linked to nature, less completely integrated into civilization and the
cultural order, than men. Men are rational agents, makers of order and
measure, controllers of history; women are emotional vessels, subjects
of orders and measures, passive observers of history. No one describes
this more clearly or more influentially for modern psychology than Sigmund Freud, who writes:

The fact that women must be regarded as having little sense of justice is no doubt
related to the predominance of envy in their mental life; for the demand for justice
is a modification of envy and lays down the condition subject to which we can lay
envy aside. We also regard women as weaker in their social interests and as having less capacity for sublimating their instincts than men.[18]

Freud subsumes women into the domain of the natural, where instinct
rules and justice is foreign.

Now, if man is to mind as woman is to body, as appears from much of
the literature and iconography of Western culture throughout historical
time, and if we adhere to a generally Cartesian view of the self as a
purely mental entity, then the self of the woman becomes deeply problematic. Can women have Cartesian egos? Genuine selves? It would
appear to be impossible if woman's essence is located in the domain of
the bodily. Clearly some other and less dichotomously dualistic conception of the self must be sought.

The associations between woman and body in Western culture have
had a decidedly negative aspect, which feminist critics have stressed.
The reduction of a woman's value to the culturally inscribed value of a
certain feminine appearance and protest against that reduction have
been strong themes of feminist criticism for several decades. Nevertheless, the appearance obsession which women are encouraged to
develop in our culture, according to which a more-or-less single standard of feminine beauty applies to all women, no matter their age, race,
build, or life-style, is as strong as ever and, some argue, gaining
strength.[19] In addition now to being slim, youthful, cosmetically
adorned to the correct degree, fashionably dressed, and as light-

skinned as possible (with of course a healthy tan to indicate white-skinned class-privilege), women must ideally have "hard bodies" with muscle-definition acquired by hours of grueling workouts and aerobic routines. That this formula cannot be met by the poor, those who don't have the time to devote to the pursuit of beauty, or those whose bodies resist the mold for whatever reason, does not mean that the standard does not hold its pristine severity over all women's heads equally. (Sadly, the appearance obsession does seem to be extending to men as well, but still seems to pertain to them in lesser degree.)

In a recent classroom discussion of trends in advertising, one young female student spoke out with sincere enthusiasm: "I can't wait till I get older! I'm going to eat whatever I want, wear whatever I want, and just not care!" An older female student turned to her and said, "Why wait? It isn't any easier to look different at age fifty than at age twenty." This exchange was instructive in many ways. There was anger in the second woman's voice; she heard herself as older being dismissed somehow from the class of viable potential beauties. There was a strange assumption behind the first woman's statements, to the effect that until some unspecified age, women are under an obligation to eat and to dress in ways other than those they would choose if not constrained. And there was in the second speaker's choice of the word *different* to describe an undisciplined woman the implicit admission that the *norm,* what it means to be *non*different, is precisely the cultural ideal of the dieting and carefully dressed youthful appearance. But this is clearly false, as a simple glance at the immense variety of actual women's bodies in any real-life situation will immediately confirm. The so-called *norm* is in fact extremely rare. Yet an enormous amount of women's energy is devoted to its pursuit. Constant dieting, eating disorders such as anorexia and bulimia, compulsive exercising, and (not least of all) enormous cash investments in beauty and fashion, are all symptomatic of the power of the cultural ideal.

To connect with our previous discussion of the gendered distinction between mind and body, men generally do not in our culture tend to identify themselves and their worth as persons with the details of their physical bodies' appearances. While in recent years the standards of male attractiveness have undoubtedly become more exacting, men clearly feel more relaxed about not meeting these standards.

Let us summarize the contribution which the dualistic Platonic–Cartesian model of the self has made to our cultural conceptions of body and mind: (1) The body's relationship to the mind, in any given human being, is one of unruly bondage or servitude; mind properly dominates its body and directs its actions, while body properly obeys. (2) Mind's behavior and dispositions are, however, described in terms more appropriate to masculine gender identity (activity, ruling or hegemony, capacity for abstraction and objectivity, distanced contemplation, dispassionate analysis), while body's configurations tend toward the feminine (passivity, subordination, unconscious physicality, sensuous and emotional implication, confusion). (3) Thus, while rationality becomes defined as a mostly masculine project, an adorned and disciplined physicality becomes the feminine project—leading to the contemporary obsession of middle-class women with weight and appearance generally. Women are given the cultural prescription to be docile bodies, adorned and available for participation in the rational schemes of the male-dominated social order. Thus the fact that in some basic respects the Cartesian ego is a masculine ego can be seen to have enormous reverberations throughout modern life. It is of no small significance to recognize that a certain outlook in the philosophy of mind provides a perfect recipe for male dominance and women's subordination.

Several important qualifications need to be made here, however. First, the neat gender dichotomy we have drawn in the ratio of proportion:

Male:Mind::Female:Body

does not appear to hold cross-racially. That is, nonwhite males in a white-dominated culture will be treated in much the same way as bodies are treated by minds in the Cartesian framework: They will be dominated, ruled, directed, used. Furthermore, white females will participate in this domination and rule, functioning as "minds" in a bureaucratic manner; and white women will benefit from skin privilege at the expense of the dominated nonwhite men and women.[20] The non-white populations will be accorded *mental* attributes that correspond to the physical attributes of the body in the Cartesian scheme; they will be considered less than fully rational, emotional, "natural" or savage, sensuous, weak-willed, and so forth. So the factor of race does much to complicate a mind–body value map which takes *only* gender into account.[21] This has led some feminist philosophers to hypothesize that *both* sexism and racism are more about power than they are about either sex or race.

A second qualification concerns the relationship between what, for want of a clearer word, we could call ideology and social reality. The rational man and the physical woman, intellectual masculinity and corporeal femininity, are creatures of ideology. This means that they are intensely value-laden concepts structuring culture and its expectations, rather than empirical generalizations drawn from observation of real women and real men. But ideology and reality touch one another at multiple points and reciprocally influence each other at these points of contact. It may be a strange-sounding philosophical thesis that rationality has been interpreted in terms defined as masculine, but it takes on a gruesomely real shape when a Berkeley philosophy professor announces to his classes that women can't do logic, or when another philosophy professor writes to the secretary of the American Philosophical Association that white women and black people of both sexes display analytical capabilities inferior to those of white men.[22] This is ideology shaping social reality with a vengeance.

Believing that the drastic dualism of the traditional picture of body's relation to mind, along with the inbuilt evaluatively hierarchical model of dominance and subordination which gives the model its working directives, are both deeply flawed, feminist philosophers look for alternatives.

A beginning point is to conceive of the human self as intrinsically embodied: An *embodied self* can displace the only questionably embodied Cartesian ego, the uncomfortably body-trapped Platonic soul, as a foundation for further inquiry into the nature of human experience. To conceive of the self as essentially or intrinsically embodied means to acknowledge the centrality of the physical in human psychology and cognition, for one thing. It means opening the door to the possibility of a bodily wisdom, to revaluing the physical human being, in ways that promise both better metaphysical schemes and more ethical models for human interaction. Breaking down the valuational hierarchy between mind and body, attempting to think of them as woven and melded together into what constitutes who we are and who we ought to be, eliminates the perhaps primary internal oppression model of mind over body. As a culture, however, we have learned to think of the body, and of those primarily identified with it, in terms of scorn (even when those latter people are ourselves). We have learned to privilege the "rational" over the emotional (conceived as proceeding from physical sources), the basely corporeal, the manual and tactile; to weigh technorationality over the mute testimony of nature and our own bodies. Those of us who are women have at times been encouraged to view our bodies with contempt when we perceive them as falling short of the beauty ideal or when we are addressed rudely in sexual terms by strangers.[23] How can we begin to approach the relation of mind and body not as a *problem* but as a source of liberatory insight and joy?

French feminist philosophers, building on their national intellectual tradition, which placed the phenomenology of *lived experience* at center stage, have made exciting progress in constructing the basis for a liberatory philosophy of the body. They have argued that the dominant tradition in Western philosophy has made women's bodies problematic in two contradictory ways: In one way, woman and body are equated as essentially physical, and women's entire personalities become sexualized (think of the late Victorian habit of referring to women as a group with the phrase "the sex," as if men were "the nonsex"). In another direction, however, the sexualized woman is either ignored in philosophy, so complete is her subsumption under the rubric *Nature*, or she is philosophized about in male terms, and her (now highlighted in neon) sexuality is described in terms appropriate only to a certain specific cultural construction of *male* sexuality. She is thus obscured as a subject, discussed as an object.

This means that, for a genuinely liberatory philosophy of the body to be developed, women must reclaim in theory and in practice their own physicality, their own sexuality. Building on the centrality of Eros and the power of sexual desire posited by Michel Foucault and Herbert Marcuse, among others, French feminist thinkers such as Luce Irigaray, Helene Cixous, and others seek to displace male philosophers' understandings of women's sexual and erotic energy with a genuinely feminine and feminist understanding. For example, human sexuality has been misleadingly described as directional and goal-oriented, with genital focus and climax the "end," and this appears to be a male-modeled way of understanding it.

Luce Irigaray suggests the at-first-sight surprising alternative view of women's sexuality that "Woman has sex organs just about everywhere."[24] The initial strangeness of this claim lies in the fact that we think of "sex organs" as those body parts most immediately involved in heterosexual copulation. But in fact, sexuality is far more pervasive throughout human experience than this view leads us to suppose. Women's erotic capacities are diffuse, multiple, and multiform rather than focused, singular, and in a phallic mode uniform. The suppression of this feminine erotic diversity can result only in the stultification of women and the impoverishment of human sexual experience generally.

Creating new understandings of women's erotic nature(s), defining our sexuality for ourselves rather than accepting stale cultural directives about it, brings with it the possibility of a new understanding of women's embodiment. Iris Marion Young has written of specific aspects of woman's embodiment that generate experiences not available to men and hence are not touched on in traditional philosophy: the feeling of having breasts, the experiences of pregnancy, childbirth. In Young's view, an attentive phenomenology of women's embodiment, of what it feels like to be a woman, yields a view of the self as multiple, flexible, and other-inclusive. For example, Young writes: "Pregnancy . . . reveals a paradigm of bodily experience in which the transparent unity of the self dissolves and the body attends positively to itself at the same time that it enacts its projects."[25]

The distinctions between inner and outer, self and other, identity and difference are all transcended in pregnancy and childbirth. Feminist metaphysics must be capable of accommodating the flexibility of these traditionally rigid distinctions. I would add that, if pregnancy is not experienced as a reality in an individual woman's life, it is frequently regarded as a possibility: to be warded off, ended, or sought, but not to be ignored. Thus many women (and this holds true for both heterosexuals and lesbians) live every day with the attendant *thought* of themselves transformed into drastically different selves (pregnant, then mother of a child), an alien imaginary for which men must appeal to science fiction or other fantastical scenarios. A feminist conception of personal identity will take in this possibility of metamorphosis, of the nearness of the strange. (In Chapter Four we explore the deeply significant ethical implications of these considerations.)

Pascal's well-known statement that "the heart has its reasons which reason does not comprehend" might well stand as the slogan for feminist philosophies of the body. We would need to point out, however, that reason's failure to comprehend the body's indigenous rationale might be more a function of reason's (read: Western philosophy's) lack of interest so far than of anything intrinsically incomprehensible in the heart's utterance of them. A philosophy of the *embodied self* will proceed from the living and desiring heart of the human person in all her specificity, through a revitalized conception of identity and sexuality, toward affirmation of liberatory prospects as yet unseen.

FOR FURTHER READING

Bordo, Susan. *The Flight to Objectivity: Essays on Cartesianism and Culture*. Albany: SUNY Press, 1987.

Garry, Ann. "Why are Love and Sex Philosophically Interesting?," *Metaphilosophy 11* (1980): 165–177.

Griffiths, Morwenna. "Feminism, Feelings, and Philosophy," *Feminist Perspectives in Philosophy*, ed. Morwenna Griffiths and Margaret Whitford. Bloomington: Indiana University Press, 1988. Pp. 131–151.

Grosz, Elizabeth (guest ed.). Special issue on feminism and the body of *Hypatia: Journal of Feminist Philosophy 6* (3) (1991).

Keller, Evelyn Fox. "The Gender/Science System: Is Sex to Gender as Nature Is to Science?," *Hypatia 2* (1987): 37–49.

Lange, Lynda. "Sexist Dualism: Its Material Sources in the Exploitation of Reproductive Labor;" *Praxis International 9* (1990): 400–407.

LeDoeuff, Michelle. "Ants and Women, or Philosophy Without Borders;" *Philosophy 21* (1987 supplementary volume): 41–54.

LeDoeuff, Michelle. *The Philosophical Imaginary.* Stanford, Calif.: Stanford University Press, 1990.

Moi, Toril (ed.). *French Feminist Thought.* Oxford: Basil Blackwell, 1987.

Overall, Christine. *Ethics and Human Reproduction.* Boston: Allen & Unwin, 1987.

Tuana, Nancy. "The Weaker Seed: The Sexist Bias of Reproductive Theory;" *Hypatia 3* (1988):35–59.

Whitbeck, Caroline. "A Different Reality: Feminist Ontology," in *Beyond Domination*, ed. Carol Gould. Totowa, N.J.: Rowman & Allanheld, 1984, Pp. 64–88.

Young, Iris Marion. *Throwing Like a Girl and Other Essays in Feminist Philosophy and Social Theory.* Bloomington: Indiana University Press, 1990.

Zita, Jacquelyn. "The Pre-Menstrual Syndrome: Dis-easing the Female Cycle;" *Hypatia 3* (1988):77–99.

CHAPTER FOUR

EPISTEMOLOGY: CRITIQUE AND CONSTRUCTION

Traditional philosophy places theories of knowledge, or *epistemologies,* among its central concerns. There is a great deal of diversity among epistemologies, but certain general tendencies have historically been prominent. In this chapter we examine three traditionally prominent epistemological dispositions, or outlooks on knowledge: rationalism, empiricism, and naturalized epistemology. The first two embrace more or less closely many of the historically canonical philosophers of the West, while the last takes in canonical philosophers not included under either a rationalist or an empiricist rubric and is, moreover, quite a popular outlook today. Detailed analyses of these will not be possible within the scope of this volume, so we must content ourselves with sketches.

We then examine some of the ways feminist philosophers have criticized each of these positions. Finally we look at three feminist epistemologies, all with many contemporary adherents and offering exciting alternatives to philosophy's epistemological tradition.

SOME EPISTEMOLOGICAL ATTITUDES

Rationalism

Our investigations of the preceding chapter into Descartes' *Meditations* and the doubt-program we saw pursued there stand us in good stead for describing rationalism, for Descartes is a card-carrying member of this epistemological group. His yearning for *certainty*, his exacting criteria concerning which beliefs can be considered certain (beyond the shadow of a doubt), and his consequent restriction of the domain of the strictly knowable to the truths of mathematics and logic, along with the fact of his own existence as a point of consciousness in an otherwise uncertainly present universe, all are virtual trademarks of rationalism.

For a rationalist, the paradigm case of a knowledge situation is one in which purely conceptual entities are investigated by an equally pure mind unfettered by sense perception with its potential inaccuracies, abstracted from the domain of the physical with its transience and fluidity. Among cognitive activities that promise to fulfill this paradigm, of course, mathematics stands foremost: Its objects are eternal yet undeniably real (say most mathematicians), and no vast amount of sense perception could have the slightest effect on the validity of a line of mathematical reasoning. Here is British mathematician G. H. Hardy describing how pure mathematics compares with less august sciences:

A chair or a star is not in the least what it seems to be; the more we think of it, the fuzzier its outlines become in the haze of sensation which surrounds it; but "2" or "317" has nothing to do with sensation; and its properties stand out more clearly the more closely we scrutinize it . . . and not because our minds are shaped in one way rather than another, but *because it is so*, because mathematical reality is built that way.[1]

This is a perfect manifesto of rationalism. The most knowable things (truths of arithmetic, logical rules, internal mental events such as spots of color on my visual field or the immediacy of my conviction that I exist) generate a hierarchy of knowledge contenders. Less knowable things (the existence of other minds, biological or psychological facts, whether the future will resemble the past) are ranked or graded according to the degree to which they either (a) can be rendered mathematical; or (b) in themselves already *resemble* the prime candidates for knowledge. So, for example, Spinoza heroically attempted to render the entire experienced and experienceable universe deductively and mathematically explainable, to show that nothing in life escapes the net of lucid certainty and logical necessity. This is to accept the rationalist's paradigm for objects of cognition but to deny that anything ultimately fails to match that criterion. Other rationalists, Plato for example, were content to cut off large portions of the universe from the domain of the knowable and to maintain that only that portion of any given thing which is directly traceable to some eternal and immutable concept or entity, a Form or Idea, can be truly known. Knowledge consists, then, in the accurate abstraction of the intelligible form from its stupefying sensual hull, like the extraction of precious metal from slag.

Stephen Jay Gould has argued that rationalism remains a potent force in the prestige ranking of different branches of science, in which those sciences which have most to do with sense experience and "hands-on" research are of lowest status, while those having the most mathematical, highly abstract, and esoteric subjects and methods (such as astrophysics) have an elite status. He maintains that the choices of research agendas in all sciences are influenced by a desire (conscious or unconscious) to conform to those of the high-status researchers. Gould quotes a physicist friend who stated in an interview with *The New York Times*, "I don't like to say bad things about paleontologists, but they're not really very good scientists. They're more like stamp collectors".[2] Thus philosophy once again bequeaths a legacy of unfortunate and stultifying prejudice. Academic philosophy, however, benefits from the prejudice in favor of "purely" intellectual cognitive activities, which is also a rationalist legacy; it still has a certain aristocratic aura, though this may be fast fading, and to identify oneself as a professor of philosophy can still provoke reactions of slightly resentful defensiveness in academic colleagues from other disciplines. Thanks to the rationalists, it is possible that academic philosophers are the astrophysicists of the liberal arts.

In any case, it is important to note by way of summary that rationalist epistemologies generate hierarchies among the knowables, that the principles of these hierarchies are determined by cognitive content resembling that of mathematics, and that knowing is paradigmatically pure intellection, the mind operating on the homey territory of that which most resembles its own rational essence. We should add that, for such an epistemology, all human rational essences are fundamentally similar in structure, so that universal validity can be expected of well-justified knowledge claims. Hence the timelessness and intersubjectively valid scope of genuine knowledge. This basic similarity of structure across all people, coupled with the fact that not all people's rational capacities function equally well or with equal dedication to cognitive pursuits, both explains and justifies the epistemological expert. This is the person who, no matter what the field of expertise, has developed the capacity to know *well* and can function as a guide to others. The well-reasoned epistemic claims of the expert have validity for all, for while all knowing is essentially the same, some are hyperknowers and have the position, even the responsibility, to inform nonhypers of their conclusions.[3]

Empiricism

By contrast with rationalism, an empiricist epistemology takes observation of actual entities in the physical world as its basic starting point and posits the primacy of sense perception in the cognitive project. The empiricist hopes to show how human belief structures are built up out of individual perceptual acts, which when combined form our sense experience. Wide variation exists among empiricist epistemologies in accounting for the combinations and orderings of individual percepts. Hume, for example, proposes a mechanism by which the percepts in a way *sort themselves* into relationships based on similarity, temporal proximity, and so forth. Others propose innate mental categories, like pigeonholes in antique desks, into which correctly sized percepts distribute themselves to form concepts by aggregation.

But crucial to the empiricist's epistemic attitude is the belief that careful and thorough observation, by a sufficiently open-minded potential knower, will eventually produce knowledge. The world presents its more or less guileless face to the investigator, and this person searches it carefully and records faithfully what is there to be seen—the knower as faithful scribe. Organized knowledge pursuits such as the individual sciences make their progress through the aggregation and correct organization of data, with subsequent formation of theories to explain these data. Since prejudice and influence by preconception are also empirically confirmable phenomena, and no observer can be said to be entirely free from them, careful potential knowers will check their results and seek confirmation in the observations of others. A sophisticated empiricism will also take cognizance of the fact that *theories* can influence observation and will be alive to the fact that theoretical commitments possibly based on someone else's erroneous observations may cloud one's present field studies. Thus backchecking on theories in the presence of divergent data is advisable.

But the basic cognitive configuration for empiricism is the clear and unwavering gaze of the observer directed toward the bland and yielding face of the observed—lacking some glitch in the program, observation yields knowledge. The face of the universe is there to be observed, recorded, and subsequently understood; its objective reality is the ontological presupposition of empiricist epistemology. While rationalism could hold its dearest knowledge claims to be true even in a vastly different kind of physical world, empiricism is bound up tightly with the objective reality of the physical world pretty much as it presents itself to unbiased sensation.

The paradigmatic knowable object for empiricists is the individual physical thing, or better still some aspect of it, which can be expressed as a "fact." Just as we saw that rationalism has its unhappy influence on the prestige ranking of the physical sciences, so empiricism finds an unhappy outlet in the social sciences during their recent mania for quantitative studies, or "number-crunching." The widespread popular belief that "you can prove anything with a survey" reflects skepticism about uncritical use of "facts" in social policy formation.

The empiricist is also committed to the possibility, and desirability, of *objectivity* in the pursuit of knowledge. Observation and contemplation of an inherently knowable universe yield intersubjectively reliable information only on the supposition that the observer or contemplator are relatively free of whatever attitudes cloud or color perception. The ideal observer is completely free of clouding and coloring prejudice, preconception, emotion, perceptual impairment of any kind. No individual human being may actually satisfy this description, but as an ideal it invites the nearest possible approximation.

Naturalized Epistemology
The tradition of naturalizing epistemology has its origin in the philosophy of Immanuel Kant (1724–1804), who maintained that the human knower actually structures cognitive experience in certain definite and

specifiable ways. What the face of the universe would look like apart from this structuring we do not and cannot know; we have access only to the structured version, and must build up our conception of what is to be known using the categories of understanding we have.

In recent epistemology, Kant's basic starting point is given an evolutionary spin by some adherents of the naturalizing program. Organisms are biologically disposed to structure their experience in those ways which give them the competitive advantage they need in the great race for survival. Human cognitive projects are to be seen in this biological context as well. Sciences and their methods are for humans what the multiple eye structure of the bee is for it — a crucially important perceptual organ which enables each organism to make its way about its environment successfully. Individual epistemic results are tested by their endurance, just as other organic developments are tested. The long neck of the giraffe is like the heliocentric theory of the solar system, or like the general disposition to trust sense perception. It works; it stays. As biological beings, humans understand the world in terms constructed by our biology. Knowledge is the more-or-less systematic representation of our interactions with the biologically structured world. Questions of whether the world is really out there, whether there are other minds perceiving it besides our own, whether we are systematically deceived, are not supposed to arise for a naturalized epistemology; experience being given, the epistemologist's task is simply to explain how it happens. Many questions about knowledge traditionally regarded as philosophical become, on the naturalized view, either scientific or psychological.

FEMINIST CRITIQUES

All three of these epistemological outlooks are subject to several general criticisms from a feminist perspective. First, the rationalist, the empiricist, and the naturalizing epistemologist alike ignore the political aspects of the "knowledge game." It is not an incidental or peripheral fact that organized knowing such as constitutes the sciences, academic disciplines, and epistemology itself is now and has been in the past the prerogative of the privileged white male. The stories of Booker T. Washington and Marie Curie are inspiring and noteworthy in part because they represent startling departures from the hegemony of the white male in cognitive pursuits. The same select group has largely controlled the institutions that disseminate organized knowledge — avenues for publication, university hiring, the awarding of research grants and prizes, including the coveted Nobel. Thus, although in the above descriptions of rationalism and so forth I wrote of "human knowledge," "biological dispositions," and other apparently quite general concepts, this was misleading; for theorizing about and systematically pursuing knowledge have been much less universally human, much more like sports activities pursued at a restricted-membership country club than such generalities would lead one to suppose.

Traditional epistemologies ignore the fact that, as the old saying goes, "knowledge is power." Feminist critics give a distinctive twist to this erstwhile inspiring adage; knowledge construed as the preserve and private playground of a privileged few has given power to those few: the power to exclude, to theorize about, and to intellectually dominate the other members of the species.

For example, Trinh Minh-ha has written of the enormous cognitive power wielded by Bronislaw Malinowski in and through his anthropological investigations. Malinowski devoted considerable labor to the project of observing and describing the societies of the western Pacific islands; his *Argonauts of the Western Pacific* achieved a wide popular readership and was responsible for introducing sophisticated notions of "the native" and of "savage society" to modern European sensibilities. Even the title is instructive in that it strikes a Western classical note, for Malinowski interpreted these societies in thoroughly modern-European terms. He searched for similarities and differences in relation to the modern European man, who thus functioned as the standard of interpretation for the "native." Malinowski stated that the rationale for anthropological investigation is the prospect of learning something about "ourselves." Trinh quotes the following instructive passage from *Argonauts:*

Perhaps *man's* mentality will be revealed to *us,* and brought near, along some lines which we have never followed before. Perhaps through realizing *human* nature in a shape very distant and foreign to us, we shall have some light shed on *our* own. In this, and in this case only, we shall be justified in feeling that it has been worth *our* while to understand these natives, *their* institutions and customs . . . [Trinh's emphasis].[4]

This passage, its strange vagueness about whether the "natives" are really human or not emphasized by Trinh's highlighting of certain key terms, brings out clearly the fact that the Other is worth understanding only if this promises to contribute something to "our" projects. And "our" projects are human projects. Anthropology thus colonizes the "savage" intellectually, bringing her under a yoke of service to Western cognitive purposes. Although Malinowski is criticized for ethnocentrism by contemporary anthropologists, Trinh does not feel that a dialogue in which "White academicians accuse white academicians of being academic and ethnocentric" is likely to be very exciting.[5] The epistemological attitude of the anthropologist is fundamentally skewed: "A conversation of 'us' with 'us' about 'them' is a conversation in which 'them' is silenced. 'Them' always stands on the other side of the hill, naked and speechless, barely present in its absence."[6]

Trinh's point here is not only that the Other who is the subject of cognizant discourse but not a participant in it is being excluded or "silenced"; she also maintains that the Other, by virtue of becoming a topic among "us" who are assuming a scientific attitude of expertise and exclusivity, is destined to be misdescribed. In her own reality, the Other is "barely present"; instead she is impersonated in an appearance and a voice not her own, a phantasm of white European academics.

I bring up this example not to unfairly target anthropologists for criticism but because it provides a vivid instance of the imperialistic potential of a politically uncritical epistemology. Bringing things back to philosophy per se, we may observe that the rationalist, the empiricist, and the naturalizing epistemologist alike assume that "human cognition" can adequately be defined by a tiny and quite specific minority of the human species and that their interests as theorists of knowledge are co-extensive with the cognitive interests of humanity at large.

Rationalism, empiricism, and naturalized epistemologies alike call for and present themselves as "value-neutral" modes of thought, disinterested in the sense of having no particular stake in specific theoretical outcomes, pursuing only the truth wherever it may lie. Feminist critics tend to deny that *any* human endeavor is value-neutral in this sense. First, there are quite specific ethical and political implications of every choice we make, from the decision to order a hamburger at a restaurant to the choice of texts for a philosophy class, and on and on. Some of the implications, thankfully, are trivial and need not be agonized over; others are enor-mously serious and can be ignored only at great peril. Theories of knowledge too have their ethical and political implications. Clearly, a theory that excludes women from higher-order cognitive capacities is evaluatively and politically charged to an extreme degree, and this would still be the case even if it turned out to be true (as it almost certainly is not).

A rationalist epistemological outlook privileges certain cognitive capacities, the mathematico-logical, at the expense of others, the sensual-perceptual. We saw in Chapter Three that the tendency to identify women with the physical, men with the intellectual sides of human nature gives this privileging a gendered aspect. A rationalist epistemology thus threatens to perpetuate existing gender-dominance relations and ratify them philosophically, through its elevation of the nonphysical knowledge object to superior epistemic status and its relegation of the physical side of nature to the epistemically deviant category.

At first sight we might expect empiricism to fare better from the standpoint of feminist critique. The empiricist's disposition to take the contributions of other observers seriously in order to check bias and error has an attractively democratic sound. But the empiricist's theoretical allegiance to the ideal of objectivity has come under serious question from feminist critics.

In her now-classic article "Gender and Science" Evelyn Fox Keller argued that certain specifics of the cognitive outlook known as the scientific method are essentially (not contingently) *masculine* in nature. Objectivity, understood at its most basic as the capacity "for delineating subject from object," is very differently achieved in masculine and in feminine personality development.[7] Preserving a radical distinction between oneself and the outside world, valuing a rigid sense of personal autonomy, and experiencing a comparatively high level of anxiety about potential intrusions on that autonomy are all features of masculine personality, according to studies performed and cited by Keller. Thus it is arguable that the emphasis on objectivity we saw as a crucial feature of empiricism is a masculine preoccupation. Yet many feminist philosophers, most notably Sandra Harding, argue that resigning objectivity altogether would be a grievous loss, both for science and for common sense. They urge that, instead of giving up on objectivity, we should work to construct a less alienated conception of it that will work for feminist purposes. We will return to the controversy about objectivity in feminist epistemology in the next section.

Finally, naturalized epistemology seems to have the advantage that it alone, among the outlooks discussed, takes seriously the *physicality* of human cognitive experience. No one can accuse the evolutionary biologist of having a distaste for the bodily! Bodies abound in this world view, and, if anything, *minds* seem to take a back seat to mindless forces on the "selfish gene's" drive toward immortality. Lacking here, however, is a proper respect for the effects of cultural construction on mentality and cognition. If she is culturally instructed from an early age that women have inferior mathematical abilities, a woman not surprisingly tends to develop inferior mathematical abilities. There seems no reason to seek any evolutionary message in this outcome. As knowers we are not only biological but also *historical* beings; our cognitive activities are carried out and take the forms they do in a specific cultural context. The language of evolutionary biology is itself a specific twentieth-century scientific dialect; it may as such capture some important truths about human existence, but it is hard to imagine that it can handle them all or will persist through the centuries as the single correct vocabulary for cognition.

Michelle Le Doeuff has written about a peculiar feeling she gets when she opens certain works of canonical philosophy:

. . . I open a work by Hegel or Leibnitz. And I catch myself thinking: "what a cheek all the same! You must have an incredible nerve to claim intellectual mastery of all that is in heaven and earth—and in human practice. A woman would never dare."[8]

This "incredible nerve," manifest especially in works of philosophy which, like Hegel's or Leibniz's, purport to offer explanations of "all that is," is an extreme example of the nerve inherent in most of traditional Western epistemology. What it means to know, who are the knowers, and what counts as an object of knowledge are all defined by a highly restrictive community. That the definitions are various has been philosophy's saving grace; opening up the membership criteria for the knowledge community is the feminist philosopher's goal.

FEMINIST EPISTEMOLOGIES

While they differ widely from one another in many respects, all feminist theories of knowledge begin from the ground-level awareness of two facts stressed above: First, both *knowing itself* and *thinking about knowing* (producing epistemologies) are activities embedded in complex networks of politics and power, these networks themselves requiring understanding and dictating caution. Second, there is widespread agreement that the dominant theories of knowledge provided by the Western philosophical tradition have focused on a specific *kind* of knowledge which is, as Lorraine Code has described it, "a commodity of privilege."[9] Asking such questions as "How do I know that there is a cat on the mat?" assumes that any "I" might be substituted for any other, that conditions of knowing are homogeneous and can be generally specified. All potential knowers have a presumed equal access to the view of the cat, and the epistemologist's job is to explain what is going on in their viewing and whether it amounts to knowledge or something else. But the fact of the matter is that ideal viewing conditions simply do not obtain for all potential viewers; in our society, knowledge conditions are vastly different for members of groups differentiated by gender, race, class, age, economic status, and so forth.

An aged woman who cannot get out to see her social worker, or who fears going downtown on the bus alone, will be ignorant of important benefits to which she may be entitled; in this sense, she will not be in a position to view that particular cat on its mat.[10] Traditional epistemologies have not regarded such situations as problematic or interesting; they have not regarded them at all. Yet surely these are situations in which the social and situational *differences* among knowers are crucial for determining the kind of knowing that can take place. Epistemologies that do not have room for these differences doom themselves to irrelevance at best, and at worst they perpetuate injustice—for, as we have already stressed, knowledge *is* power.

We will now examine three current feminist epistemologies and explore the extent to which they succeed in transcending the limitations of their privilege-oriented predecessors. The epistemologies we will take up are feminist empiricism, feminist-standpoint theory, and postmodernist epistemology. All represent complex positions that can only be presented in outline here; again, though, the reader who wishes to explore any position in greater depth is referred to the For Further Reading section at the end of this chapter.

Feminist Empiricism

As feminists look back on the history of Western philosophy they find much to either shock, anger, or amuse them, depending on their frame of mind: grossly sexist, trivializing, and infantilizing descriptions of "the nature of Woman"; expansive claims about the "production of the State" in which women's labors and contributions are negated; ignorantly false claims about women's biology, moral character, and intellect; fatuous and class-biased assertions about "women's place"; wishful claims implying that all women are heterosexual and furthermore need men to complete their lives, and (alas) more.

One way to react to all this is that prescribed by the feminist empiricist, who suggests that philosophy's shortcomings with regard to white women, to women and men of color, to lesbians, and to all the nonprivileged, can be remedied by a more careful adherence to what is after all philosophy's stated mission: the pursuit of wisdom, the search for truth. What has produced the lamentably flawed history of philosophy has been a pattern of failures to live up to the basic scenario of empiricist knowing: the unbiased observation of the face of the universe. Prejudice and bias have been all too clearly present, clouding the judgement of the philosopher and skewing the resultant description.

To give just one famous example: Aristotle, whose allegiance to careful empirical observation is stated and evinced everywhere in his work, is incorrect about the number of teeth women have. He asserts that the adult man has thirty-two teeth but the adult woman only twenty-eight. Now, this cannot have been a function of the difficulty of observation, as women with countable teeth existed in plenty then as now. Rather, scholars have hypothesized that Aristotle counted the teeth in the male jaw and, in the grip of a powerful prejudice, subtracted four to arrive at the number in a woman's (smaller) jaw. Another possibility is that he observed the dentition of a woman who had no wisdom teeth. In either case, Aristotle's mistake is a result of failing to be a *good enough empiricist* rather than something endemic to the method of observation itself.

The feminist empiricist maintains that philosophers and scientists need to be told to "Look again!" rather than to find a wholly new way of looking. The prospects for a better philosophical understanding of human existence and its surroundings will improve as larger numbers of women enter the domains in which "received knowledge" is processed and produced: universities, laboratories, publishing houses, journal editorial boards, and funding agencies. These women will be placed well to point out mistakes in the observations of their colleagues and to set up research agendas that promise to avoid the mistakes of the past.

Sandra Harding points out that there is a beneficial kind of "conservatism" about feminist empiricism; since it is mainly a call for *better* philosophy, *better* science, and so forth, in styles already institutionally recognized as valid, it is not in principle terribly disturbing to those who already hold positions of power and influence in the knowledge-production sites.[11] A privileged white male anthropologist, for example, is less likely to be mortally offended by a new colleague who happens to be a lesbian of color when she points out that there was a gap in his last field study (e.g., he neglected to ask the older women question X) than when she points out that his entire field methodology is flawed. He will be less threatened by *her own* work if it reflects an allegiance to the basic conception of anthropology as a science which he shares. And her survival in this workplace may well depend on her ability to blend her research methods and aims with the more traditional ones which surround her.

Alison Jaggar has argued, however, that the call to do better science, better pursuit of truth, in the traditional empiricist way may not be sufficient to dislodge the deeply ingrained tendency toward omission and distortion in received "knowledge." This is because the ideal observer of the empiricist tradition, the detached, unbiased, unprejudiced truth seeker who reads nature's face with wide-open eyes, is willfully ignorant of his or her own political and social situation (these are particulars from which abstraction is made in order to assimilate oneself to the ideal observer and thus ensure objectivity). Jaggar writes: ". . . [G]ood scientists are detached observers and manipulators of nature who follow strict methodological rules, which enable them to separate themselves from the special values, interests, and emotions generated by their class, race, sex, or unique situation."[12]

They thus resemble the "abstract individuals" of liberal political theory. This points up a problem for feminist empiricism, because (a) the feminist empiricist is committed to making knowledge which reflects and can criticize, rather than obscuring, social reality; and (b) abstract individualism has already been seen to lie at the root of many of traditional philosophy's shortcomings from a feminist perspective (see Chapter Two). Jaggar concludes that the deep conceptual link between empiricism and liberalism signals a reason for rejecting feminist empiricism.

By contrast, Lynn Hankinson Nelson has recently argued that a full and complete empiricism must go beyond individualism and generate a new, nonatomistic way of conceiving the *community* of knowers.[13] She argues, partly on conceptual grounds and partly on the basis of evidence drawn from observation of working scientists, that the extent of cooperation and collaboration in the formation of research protocols, the articulation and exploration of philosophical problems, and so forth are greater than is supposed by some critics, and that the "individualism" and "distancing" which are thought to be part of the objectivity of the ideal observer are largely rhetorical rather than real. She reasons that an accurate recognition of these facts, combined with understanding and encouragement of the collaborative aspects of knowledge-making processes in many spheres, will produce better results from a reconceived and genuinely collaborative empiricist epistemology.

Against this one might argue that, in my example of the anthropologists above, there are some unanswered questions that make the example seem artificially abstracted from its real social context; foremost among them is this: Who encouraged this lesbian of color to imagine herself in an anthropological research group some day, to choose and to pursue the rigorous educational agenda that would qualify her for such work, and finally, who hired this lesbian of color, and why? Realistic answers to these questions will have to introduce a social background which stretches far beyond the research institute's walls, for nothing less than a massive and long-lasting movement for social transformation can have made this scenario possible. The women who are entering the academy, the sciences, and (ever so slowly) the boardrooms of corporations are doing so not only because they worked very hard at becoming good knowledge-makers in the time-honored ways (though they did work very hard), but because many people for many years have been chopping away at a big tree with a small axe—to paraphrase Bob Marley. I am uncertain whether feminist empiricism can motivate the far-reaching political critique which makes both the presence of our young anthropologist in her research group, and the integrity of her research agenda, comprehensible. As Harding has written,

What we can see in the world around us is a function not just of what is there plus our individual talents and skills but of how our society designs the cultural filters through which we observe the world around and within us and how it institutionalizes those filters in ways that leave them invisible to individuals. Individual biases and differences in assumptions can be identified and eliminated by routine scientific methods, but the culturewide ones require different methods of detection. A social movement on behalf of the less advantaged groups is one such different and valuable "scientific method."[14]

Nelson's community of empiricist knowers is an intriguing proposal, and certainly deserves a good deal of further consideration. But some feminist philosophers have argued that a somewhat more radical approach than feminist empiricism is called for; we turn now to standpoint theories, which attempt to show that traditional epistemologies are not just imperfectly realized, but seriously and essentially incomplete.

Feminist-Standpoint Epistemology

We noted in Chapter One that philosophy's history has issued predominantly from the minds of privileged white males. It was suggested that their position, their standpoint, has had a decisive influence on the shape history has taken. Though many philosophers have presumed to speak for all "mankind," for "Reason itself," or even for "Absolute Spirit," and to be discussing the general "Nature of Mind," "conditions for knowledge," and "the human good," feminist critics have shown and continue to show the limitations of such spuriously universal discourse, and to point out large portions of human experience as yet undreamt of in their philosophy.

This specificity of the traditional standpoint has led some feminist philosophers to explore the potential of basing an epistemology in a feminist (sometimes in a women's) standpoint. The basic assumption, originating in a Hegelian or Marxian view that the human self is essentially shaped by its material activities and situation, is that women's lives have differed from men's lives in ways that would construct clear differences in their respective world views and self-concepts. Since the making and transmitting of knowledge are crucially important human activities, women's "ways of knowing" may be expected to be no less real than men's, but they are also quite likely to be very different from what traditional epistemology has supplied from the white men's standpoint.

Feminist-standpoint epistemologies seek to uncover and describe women's knowledge-making activities as these have originated in and been shaped by women's daily work and women's values. This project is in part discovery and in part creation, for while some aspects of women's experience readily yield epistemic material, in many dimensions women's activities have been so thoroughly relegated to the unscientific, the nonintellectual, the natural, and so forth that the epistemological scheme or belief and value structure into which they fit must be constructed.

If we look at women's work generally, attempting to keep in view cultural, historical, racial, and class differences among women, we are struck by certain recurrences: women are responsible for child care, dependent care generally, and housecleaning, in almost all cultures and almost all classes of society. Affluent women may not do the work with their own hands, but it remains their department to organize and oversee. In addition, vast numbers of women function as either paid or unpaid workers outside the home (unpaid work in communally farmed agricultural areas and care for domestic animals on subsistence farms, paid work in a shop, factory, school, corporation, etc.).[15] There are types of work which are culturally identified as "women's work," independent of the question whether all women do such work; women's work tends to be associated with caring for others, cleaning up after others, attending to the needs of others, and in addition it both carries low social status and brings low monetary or in-kind compensation (or none whatsoever).

Thus, while women's work can embrace both a private and a public sphere, already doing so for most women in most third world countries and increasingly doing so in the "first world" as well, men's work is largely located in the public spaces of the culture.[16] Women's work in the domestic sphere tends to require a high degree of interpersonal interaction, involving as it does other human beings and their welfare. Men's work takes place in more regulated situations, in which the interpersonal element typically is subordinated to some larger bureaucratically defined process and where rule-following can govern behavior.

Now, standpoint theorists in feminist epistemology look at how these different work situations (women's dual-sphere work responsibilities, men's single-sphere work responsibilities) shape personality and character along gender-specific lines. Women, to be proficient workers in both their domains, must become conversant with two different sets of behavior prescriptions: those appropriate to the domestic, personal situations in which they are caregivers and maintainers of life, and those appropriate to the more public and male-dominated locations in which they also labor. Behaviorally, then, and epistemically, they must be able to speak two languages, avail themselves of two different repertoires of rules dictating appropriate activity.[17] Even if they are choosing to flout those rules, to be bad caregivers, bad "homemakers," lazy field hands, etc., they will be conversant with the standards they are deciding *not* to meet. Men, however, will be monolingual (as it were), and their epistemic strategies will show this singularity of emphasis.

This brings out an important point concerning standpoint theories. Those who advocate the construction of a feminist-standpoint epistemology do not *merely* maintain that "adding in" this standpoint, derived from women's experiences and practices traditionally excluded from philosophy's purview, will produce better philosophy, science, politics, etc.; they go further and argue that the feminist standpoint has certain inherent epistemic *advantages* over androcentric epistemologies which make it a better place to stand, so to speak, when engaged in the making of knowledge.[18]

We can see that the duality of the kinds of work situations women face would give them a superior adaptability and a broader comprehension of the full reality of their social, political, and economic situations. In addition, their status as economic and social inferiors to the men whose lives they produce and facilitate forces them to learn to speak the dominant public language and mediate between the man's world and that part of their world which he does not share. This encourages them to develop the bridging skills, ability to mediate, capacity for viewing things from another's perspective, and translation facility across different conceptual schema which are so important not only to good knowing but to good living as well.[19]

In the popular public television series *Upstairs, Downstairs* we find a good practical illustration of the epistemic advantages of oppression. The servants' culture, downstairs in the Bellamy household, depended for its livelihood and happiness on their ability to keep things "upstairs" running smoothly and comfortably; this required considerable psychological sophistication, pooling of shreds of information, weighing of hypotheses about what had gone wrong in times of trouble, and skill in offering the right amount and kind of comfort, advice, information. The Bellamy family displayed over and over again a total lack of awareness of what things were really like "downstairs," and they could afford their ignorance; indeed, one could say they purchased the prerogative of not having to be bothered by the downstairs denizens' own complexities.

In much the same way, standpoint theorists argue, women (and men who are members of other oppressed groups) in many if not most contemporary cultures depend for their livelihood or even survival on being sensitive to the moods and dispositions of those for whom they care and those they serve. This causes them to develop perceptual capacities, communication skills, a facility for emotional management, conflict resolution, discretion, acting skill, and many other behaviors it is the privilege of the ruling class and gender to neglect. All of these skills originate in a basic ability to *relate,* to *connect* with others; to mentally negotiate that balance between one's own needs and theirs which will best serve mutual or common interests. The ethical promise of feminist standpoint theory is discussed in Chapter Five; for present purposes it suffices to concentrate on the epistemological promise. Here the feminist standpoint lends itself to a more robust objectivity than that available to the traditional epistemologist who is trapped in a white male paradigm, for women's consciousness looks at things from at least two distinct and opposed perspectives. Also, the disposition to connect with others encourages knowledge-making which will be situated, socially nuanced, and tend toward a democratic collaboration. And feminist awareness of the consequences of oppression, our knowledge of what it feels like to be erased, ignored, patronized, and brushed off as a potential knowledge-maker, cannot but encourage the development of nonoppressive, and more inclusive, knowledge-making practices.

Critics of feminist-standpoint epistemologies are not lacking. Some are concerned about the appearance of the excessive "homogenization" of women's situations statements of the position seem to display.[20] Drastic differences in women's situations exist; after all, some of the Bellamy family were women, and some women enjoy positions of such privilege relative to others that it seems an absurd stretch to bring them together in a common logical space; the traditional wife of a powerful financier may have to kowtow to his moods at times if he is her sole means of support, but does this really compare to the crushing double workday of the women who clean the high-rise buildings he owns?

Furthermore, some of the "skills" women and other oppressed groups have developed in our two-world situation work smartly against us; we have learned to dissemble, so we lie to each other; we know how to sense emotions, so we manipulate; we are ourselves sensitive, and thus we take offense easily, blow up at each other and factionalize our women's groups; we understand the mind of an oppressor, and we ourselves can therefore become skillful oppressors when the chance presents itself and we are so inclined.[21] In short, it does not do to over-romanticize what we have learned from being where we are.

However, standpoint theory is built on a basic insight which seems to me compelling: It would be hard to argue against the claim that experience importantly structures our cognitive capacities, determining which ones we will work hard to develop and which we will ignore. And because epistemology has been the project of one small and comparatively homogeneous group, it will revolutionize and liberate epistemological thinking and knowledge-making itself to look and listen carefully to the knowledge-construction projects of those who have so far been left out, relegated to the category of "known" rather than invited and encouraged to see themselves as "knowers."

Indeed, standpoint epistemologies are developed not only by and for women as a group, but by and for lesbians, and by and for black women, and by and for American Indian women. We have seen black and American Indian feminist standpoint theories in Chapter One and examine a lesbian-standpoint ethics in Chapter Five.

Postmodern Epistemologies

The terms *postmodern* and *postmodernism* have appeared abundantly in recent scholarly literature from a variety of disciplinary backgrounds but, strangely enough, they are seldom defined. This is all the more curious in that the sense of the term *modern* is far from clear; in standard philosophy course offerings, students are surprised to find that Modern Philosophy courses begin with Descartes and typically conclude with Kant (late eighteenth century). Postmodernism seems to denote a state of mind rather than a time period; the postmodern state of mind is one in which we are affected by what Jane Flax has described as "profound yet little comprehended change, uncertainty, and ambivalence" about the achievements and intellectual highlights of Western civilization.[22]

Flax points to certain specific historical events as catalysts of this crisis of confidence: the Holocaust, nuclear warfare past and possibly future, and the Vietnam war are perhaps the most significant. Taken together, these have dislodged many of the cherished beliefs of Western culture: the belief in a benevolent human Reason which progresses toward enlightenment in gradual but incremental steps; the belief in Science as a saving force and as a paradigm for all true knowledge; the belief in the autonomous and stable human Self as the linchpin of political order and the free pursuer of the Good. These beliefs, now shaken loose from our hands, were our legacy from the European intellectual and scientific optimists of the seventeenth and eighteenth centuries, the Age of Enlightenment. History, combined with the "deconstructing" work of such thinkers as Nietzsche, Wittgenstein, Derrida, Foucault, Rorty, and Lyotard, has smashed this belief system; hence we are a culture "in crisis."[23]

Postmodern philosophers take as their task the *deconstruction* (careful critical analysis to reveal grossly problematic assumptions and contradictions) of philosophical concepts and positions which they feel are implicated in the world view of "modernity." Modernity too reveals itself to be a state of mind rather than a historical time period; it is that state of mind in which we looked to specialists of various kinds, such as scientists, philosophers, and elite artists to preserve and save us—to interpret us to ourselves and place us in categories ("Better living through chemistry," slogan of the DuPont Corporation during the late 1950s, for example). We were confident that such salvation was forthcoming, first to the deserving peoples of the triumphant West, subsequently and in much the same form to the more "backward" but eventually equally autonomous and free peoples of the third world.

To feminist philosophers, postmodernism has promised the most thorough and radical destruction of traditional binary gender thinking of any intellectual tradition so far manifest. The deconstruction of dualisms is a fundamental practice of the postmodern thinker, who attempts to demonstrate how one side of any opposition inevitably collapses into its supposed opposite upon any deep understanding of either.

Also appealing for feminist purposes is postmodernism's intense polemic against universalizing in any form. We have seen how philosophers easily fall into the habit of speaking for "all mankind"; this habit is not theirs alone, however. Throughout our written culture, and in feminist thinking too, we find this old bad habit hard to break; Elspeth Probyn writes of "the ontological conceit of the western subject" as an ingrained attitude detectable in even quite careful and crossculturally literate feminist thinking.[24]

Feminist postmodern epistemologies are thus essentially critical. Only through a thoroughgoing deconstruction of "our intellectual heritage" (every word of which phrase should be questioned), an abjuring of privileged standpoints and claims to objective truth, and a relentless critique of the relation between knowledge-making and power-guarding can a liberatory feminist thinking and practice proceed.

In the absence of objective truth, epistemically privileged standpoints, methodologies legitimated by experts, and all the other apparatus of traditional knowledge-seeking, what will make any knowledge claim more reliable than any other? Is this epistemic anarchism, a situation in which all claims, no matter how bizarre or contradictory, are equally valid? Postmodern feminist epistemologies maintain that knowledge claims will find all the legitimation they need in "localized practices," in the application they find in contexts socially and historically specific, for which they were designed.[25] Thus what will emerge is a kind of *epistemic pluralism,* similar to that seen in the lesbian epistemologies of Chapter Two; the knowledge I need will be made by me, and those immediately surrounding me, in the work we do; it will be circulated to the extent that others' practices encourage such interaction, and will grow or change in this interactive process. What I must not do is dictate in advance the shape this knowledge must take (rational, empirical, justifiable under counterfactual test, etc.) or impose this knowledge on anyone else in some kind of intellectual imperialist frenzy.

Here we can see the strong influence of the philosophy of American pragmatism, which has only recently been recognized as an important potential contributor to feminist thought.[26]

Some feminist philosophers express serious concerns about post-modernism as a viable basis for epistemology or for feminist politics in general.[27] If a radical deconstruction of gender categories is carried out, where is the basis for the claim that women as such have anything in common? If gender identity is revealed to be an entirely social construct, a myth told to serve the interests of the lords of culture, where is the basis for feminist thinking? Sisterhood is *not* powerful if it is merely a bad dream caused by some foul cognitive substance we ingested last millennium.

Sandra Harding has expressed concern that the willingness to resign objectivity and individual autonomy to the dustbin of outmoded obsessions is perhaps a luxury many feminists would not afford. Western academic women have "had access to the benefits of the Enlightenment" and thus might give them up more easily than other women, especially third-world women, who have yet to achieve the political autonomy, suffrage and legal rights, and degree of access to the benefits of science their Western sisters enjoy.[28] Thus it is all too easy for Western feminists to criticize the philosophical foundations on which liberalism and modern science rest; such critical latitude is born of privilege.[29]

There are also good reasons for caution about the relinquishing of the concept of objectivity as understood by Western science. Many of the most significant advances in women's political history have been achieved through successfully putting across the argument that barriers to women's freedom are based only on prejudice, a mistaken and subjective attitude. Appeals to fairness, justice, and dispassionate objectivity have been powerful elements in this argument. Most of us believe that sexism, racism, heterosexism, and other pernicious attitudes are not objectively defensible, are based in part on false beliefs and bad faith or moral inconsistency. If we no longer have a standpoint from which to make these claims, with what justification can we continue to decry the attitudes? We ought rather to seek to reconceive the notions of objectivity, justice, and truth than to discard them and leave ourselves rhetorically helpless.

Finally, my own criticism of postmodern feminist epistemologies stems from a disturbing feeling that the critical and deconstructive spirit can become intoxicated with its *own* power, becoming a nihilistic and destructive force which sweeps all before it like dry leaves before a harmattan wind. Consider the following statements from Jane Flax: given that Western culture is in crisis, feminists must work to ". . . further decenter the world. . . . If we do our work well, reality will appear even more unstable, complex, and disorderly than it does now. In this sense, perhaps Freud was right when he declared that women are the enemies of civilization."[30]

My fear is that, in an increasingly decentered, unstable, disorderly and uncivilized world, raw power will be the only arbiter of right. Those most vulnerable in our present world, however fragile its order, would be the first to suffer under such conditions.

Yet, if we can formulate some controls over the critical spirit, we can recognize the enormous potential contribution of postmodernist feminism to epistemological projects; if nothing else, the postmodernist agenda will be an ever-present lesson in humility and caution against the "ontological conceits" to which we have shown ourselves so consistently attracted in the past.

In summary, much creative ferment in feminist epistemology can be seen. For all their differences, all three of the types of feminist epistemology which we have observed are committed to several common and readily identifiable aims:

1. All seek to highlight, and ultimately to reform in a liberatory way, the relationship between knowledge-making and power-holding within cultures.

2. All seek to open the doors of the institutions which create and process received knowledge to those traditionally excluded from those spaces.

3. All are committed to (2) above, not only because considerations of social justice would warrant such inclusion but also because it is a consequence of their epistemic premises that *better knowledge for everyone* will be the result.

FOR FURTHER READING

Bleier, Ruth. *Science and Gender: A Critique of Biology and Its Theories on Women*. New York: Pergamon Press, 1984.

Butler, Judith. *Gender Trouble: Feminism and the Subversion of Identity*. New York: Routledge, 1989.

Code, Lorraine. "Is the Sex of the Knower Epistemologically Significant?;" *Metaphilosophy 12* (1981):267–276.

Code, Lorraine. *What Can She Know? Feminist Theory and the Construction of Knowledge*. Ithaca, N.Y.: Cornell University Press, 1991.

Flax, Jane. *Thinking Fragments: Psychoanalysis, Feminism, and Postmodernism in the Contemporary West*. Berkeley: University of California Press, 1989.

Fraser, Nancy. *Unruly Practices: Power, Discourse, and Gender in Contemporary Social Theory*. Minneapolis: University of Minnesota Press, 1989.

Harding, Sandra. *The Science Question in Feminism*. Ithaca, N.Y.: Cornell University Press, 1986.

Harding, Sandra. *Whose Science? Whose Knowledge?* Ithaca, N.Y.: Cornell University Press, 1991.

Heldke, Lisa. "Recipes for Theory Making;" *Hypatia 3* (1988):15–29.

Holler, Linda. "Thinking with the Weight of the Earth: Feminist Contributions to an Epistemology of Concreteness;" *Hypatia 5* (1990):1–23.

Hubbard, Ruth. "Science, Facts, and Feminism;" *Hypatia 3* (1988): 5–17.

Jaggar, Allison M., and Susan R. Bordo (eds.). *Gender/Body/Knowledge: Feminist Reconstructions of Being and Knowing.* New Brunswick, N.J.: Rutgers University Press, 1989.

Jaggar, Allison M. "Love and Knowledge: Emotion in Feminist Epistemology;" *Inquiry 32* (1989): 151–176. Reprinted in *Gender/Body/Knowledge*, eds. Susan Bordo and Allison M. Jaggar. New Brunswick, N.J.: Rutgers University Press, 1989.

Longino, Helen. *Science as Social Knowledge: Values and Objectivity in Scientific Inquiry.* Princeton, N.J.: Princeton University Press, 1990.

Nelson, Lynn Hankinson. *Who Knows? From Quine to a Feminist Empiricism.* Philadelphia: Temple University Press, 1990.

Poovey, Mary. "Feminism and Deconstruction;" *Feminist Studies 14* (1988): 51–65.

Winant, Terry. "The Feminist Standpoint: A Matter of Language;" *Hypatia 2* (1987): 123–148.

Whitbeck, Caroline. "Love, Knowledge, and Transformation;" *Hypatia 2* (1987): 393–405.

CHAPTER FIVE

ETHICS IN FEMINIST PERSPECTIVE

Since many of the basic issues in feminism are ethical issues, it is not surprising that a tremendous amount of feminist energy has been devoted to moral thinking, to opening up and following new lines of moral debate. Feminist critique of the moral-philosophical tradition has, of course, been intense and diverse, but certain common themes emerge: Much moral philosophy has tended to obscure, rather than clarify or at least honestly acknowledge, its political basis and implications; much moral philosophy has employed an atomistic and individualistic concept of the self; and much moral philosophy has either explicitly or implicitly derogated the activities and concerns of women to second-class status. But, as in the other areas of philosophy so far examined, in ethics as well feminist thought has gone far beyond critique in constructive ways.

In some cases, this has led to reinterpretation of the moral theories of traditional philosophers, in the belief that they offer useful material for feminist interests. Mainstream philosophers such as Hume, Kant, Mill, and Sartre have been "recruited" by feminist philosophers in this way, and their refurbished doctrines made the basis for a liberatory moral philosophy. In other cases more radical departures from the tradition in Western philosophical ethics have been made, introducing new methods, new problems, and new values.

In this chapter we begin by exploring the ways in which a representative mainstream moral philosophy has been criticized from a feminist perspective; an appropriate choice for this purpose is the philosophy of John Rawls. Rawls is particularly appropriate for this purpose, not because his thought is especially or egregiously biased (it isn't), but because of the enormous influence it has exerted in Anglo-American philosophical circles. Also, Rawls' philosophy is "classical" in the sense of offering quite a global account of human moral life, a sizable vision of the Good, which sits squarely within the dominant liberal tradition. It will thus serve well to illustrate the way in which feminists have taken issue with that tradition. We will then turn to the constructive efforts by feminists to create a more satisfying ethical vision.

RAWLS AND THE VEIL OF IGNORANCE

In his monumental book *A Theory of Justice* (1971) John Rawls presents a description of the basic structure of a just society, including the fundamental principles of justice which will shape and dictate that structure.[1] In order to arrive at a picture of this just society, he begins with a variation on a time-honored thought-experiment: the "social contract." Social contract theorists (among whom Rawls acknowledges as founding influences Locke, Rousseau, and Kant)[2] imagine societies being founded by committees of already mature and socialized human beings who come together in common purpose to create political systems according to their most basic physical, moral, and psychological needs. Rawls varies the traditional social contract schema in two important ways: (1) He specifies that the committee members will be unaware of their own personal talents and abilities, their "conceptions of the good," and their "special psychological propensities"; and (2) he decrees that they will have no inkling of the position they might occupy in the society they are about to structure.[3] They are thus pictured as standing behind a "veil of ignorance" whose shadow extends even to their own hearts and minds.

These variations on the traditional contract theme are intended to ensure that self-interest does not skew the conception of justice which they produce; if, for example, I could know while standing in the original position that I had big feet, I might be inclined to privilege big-footedness or big-shoe makers in some way so as to ensure myself a higher status in the "just" society. More subtly, if I could know that my personal conception of the good includes development of my rational capacities, I might be inclined (as were certain Greek philosophers) to build the intellectual virtues into the highest level of human existence or to decree that philosophers must become rulers. The veil of ignorance, then, is a device for ensuring maximum fairness in the conception of justice which will emerge.

Can those standing in the original position know their sex? In the passage just cited, Rawls does not explicitly list sex as one of the veiled traits; however, in a later article he states that it was intended to be included in the phrase *natural assets.*[4] As Susan Moller Okin has pointed out, the omission of explicit attention to sex may, however, be symptomatic of a deeper problem in the original position.[5]

For sex and the attendant gender roles and traits can hardly be considered "natural assets"; the enormously complex network of prescriptions concerning gender-appropriate behavior and values is in large part the product of a socialization process that begins soon after birth and continues throughout our lives. The veil of ignorance obscures the fact that any thinkable human adult who stands in the original position will be ignorant, not only of purely biological facts about itself but also of the more complex gender facts that maturation in a culture contributes to thought and personality.

A defender of Rawls would at this point insist that gender be superadded to sex as yet another level of traits unknown to the original position holders. Can this be done without damage to Rawls' overall project?

Feminist critics such as Okin, Annette Baier, and Seyla Benhabib have argued that the problem for Rawls which results from his disinclination to discuss sex and gender explicitly is quite profound.[6] In order for the "original-position" exercise to work, Rawls must presuppose morally mature individuals, already inclined to value fairness, to discourse with one another honestly and in an above-board way (no palace coups behind the veil),[7] and to value one another's values sufficiently to want to make a state which will allow to each individual the maximal pursuit of realization of values consistent with equal liberty for all. He is aware of this and provides an explanation of how moral maturity is achieved; in order to remain consistent with the strictures on the original position which he has set up, however, he must provide a conception of moral development which presupposes as little as possible about the actual conditions of childhood and its social framework; he must sketch a kind of moral minimum necessary to ground the psychology required for good original-position holders. The family he constructs will be both minimal (so as to presuppose as little as possible in the way of detail) and ideal (to illustrate clearly the emergence of commitment to fairness, etc. from early experiences).

And it is an extremely interesting family! It needs to produce children who will have "the sense of justice," understood as "the settled disposition to adopt and to want to act from the moral point of view insofar at least as the principles of justice define it."[8] Rawls describes three psychological laws which dictate a process of development initiated in interaction between parents and child, and culminating in the ideal citizen of the just state.

The first law explains how children come to love their parents: "First law: given that family institutions are just, and that the parents love the child and manifestly express their love by caring for his good, then the child, recognizing their evident love of him, comes to love them."[9]

Just family institutions must be presupposed for this psychological law to take effect. Justice for family institutions has, however, no adequate explanation in Rawls' theory. As Okin has argued, it is assumed at this late stage in the book, because it is needed to explain how the sense of justice enters our minds in the first place, but it is never explicated.[10]

Can we simply say that the family will be just in the same way that the society as a whole is just? In other words, should we say that the family satisfies the conception of justice if it would survive a "veil of ignorance–Original Position" thought experiment? But Rawls has blocked this move, for he has specified that the participants in the original position experiment as described are "heads of families" or "representatives of families."[11] This stunning departure from the rather naked character of the individuals behind the veil is needed, Rawls argues, in order to give some kind of minimum temporal continuity to the just society being envisioned—heads of families are pictured as concerned to some degree with some member or members of the next generation, their own child or children. Thus they provide stabilizing ballast for the continuing life of the society, precluding the possibility that, for example, a single generation of original-position holders would design a state in which all the goods are enjoyed and consumed by themselves, a hedonistic lemming culture which ignores the interests of the next generation.[12]

Since, in order to anchor concern for the next generation, Rawls suggests that the original-position holders may be thought of as heads of households, we can infer that there may be members of households whose sense of justice is not relevant to the deliberation process which goes on behind the veil. Rawls must be assuming that the head of the household will, in a familiar paternalistic way, be concerned about these unrepresented parties' interests too. But now we have ground for serious concern about the fairness that we were seeking. For in this picture, the individual is motivated by self-interest above all; Rawls states and restates his commitment to a "postulate of mutual disinterest," defined as "individuals taking no interest in one another's interests."[13] Rawls needs parent-child concern, and therefore he curbs the strength of the postulate of mutual disinterest in the way we have seen; but at this logical level he does not need concern for one's spouse or for extended family members. The paternally headed household which sends its leader to the bargaining table is a potential locus of the grossest tyranny.

Let us return to the Rawlsian family, which is training its child in the ways of justice. Once the first psychological law has been obeyed and the child has come to love its parents because they "manifestly" love the child, Rawls maintains that the "capacity for fellow-feeling" has been realized. The second and third psychological laws apply this fellow-feeling in increasingly wider circles. Again, given that social arrangements and societal institutions are just and are known to be just by all, the maturing child will acquire the developed sense of (and appreciation for) justice by seeing how it regulates interactions with others to his benefit.[14]

Here, as elsewhere in Western moral and political philosophy, the nuclear family is simply assumed. Perfect parents, loving and caring, perform unspecified ministrations which eventually encourage the child (here pictured as the kind of egoistic rational bargainer so omnipresent in recent political thought) to "love" them. This "love," completely unanalyzed and undefined, is the first chink in the child's egoistic armor, a crucial one that allows others to loom importantly on its moral horizons.

Feminist critics claim that Rawls' theory of justice gives us both too much and too little: too much, in the sense that it imports the nuclear family, the paternalistic family-head, the egoistic rational bargainer as a model human personality, and more into a scenario which is supposed to be bare of ethical specification; too little, in that it mystifies the role of sex and gender in the just society, rules out in advance the significance of basic gender differences in moral psychology, and accounts for moral development in a way that totally bypasses the kind of direct moral training which is a great part of the work of parents (historically, mainly mothers).[15] In the next section we look at attempts by feminist philosophers to escape beyond these difficulties, widespread within the Western liberal tradition, to new ethical terrain.

JUSTICE AND CARE

A recent controversy in developmental psychology raised an issue of great interest to many feminist moral philosophers. During the 1960s psychologist Lawrence Kohlberg had developed a series of tests that would measure the "moral maturity" of human subjects. Using a subject population of college students, mostly male, Kohlberg was able to differentiate a number of distinct moral stages and to rank these in a linear scale of maturity culminating in "level six," originally identified as the norm of full development but later restricted to a few and renamed "moral sainthood."[16] Kohlberg's ethical model or ideal was explicitly derived from the ethics of Immanuel Kant and highlighted such aspects as the avoidance of emotional grounds for moral action, a disposition to think in terms of general ethical principles or laws, an interest in the vocabulary of moral "justice," and the capacity for selfless or self-sacrificing behavior in the interests of humanity at large, as characteristics of a relatively high level of moral maturity. In general, one moves along Kohlberg's scale through a process of decentering the personal self from one's moral field of vision. We begin life, on this view, as unprincipled ethical egoists. Some remain this way throughout their lives; others progress by gradually deepening their commitment to more-or-less impersonal ideals such as "obeying the law," "acting for the general good," "serving mankind." Moral sainthood is achieved by those few (Gandhi, King, Mother Teresa) who devote their whole energies to the welfare of others.

Kohlberg's test had great appeal, especially in the field of education. Versions of it were adopted for classroom administration, and the general model of development it enshrined was also adopted as the basis for the "moral education" movement in American primary- and secondary-education theory.

But in the early 1980s, questions were raised about it both inside and outside developmental psychology. Inside, developmental psychologist Carol Gilligan had begun to notice small but systematic discrepancies between the moral maturity scores of men and women; the men appeared to rate slightly higher than the women, and Gilligan wondered why. To answer her questions, she initiated a woman-based (and largely woman-administered) research project designed to arrive at a characterization of women's moral reasoning processes which would not proceed from a male model (recall the male college students of Kohlberg's initial research and his allegiance to Kant) but would allow whatever is distinctive to women's own perspective to shape a possibly different paradigm of "moral maturity."

Gilligan's results, appearing for public review first in the 1981 book *In a Different Voice*,[17] showed a pattern of moral reasoning among the women studied which diverged from the Kant–Kohlberg paradigm in several distinct ways. First, women reasoning their way through a moral dilemma tended to focus on the specific personal *relationships* within which the principal agents find themselves situated. They pondered on the nature and character of these relationships, tending to derive relevant ethical considerations from specific connectedness among persons. Second, they reasoned that relationships generate *responsibilities* and that these responsibilities might be quite specific within the relationship. That is, their interest was not in a generic relationship type, such as "mother-to-child" or "lover-to-lover," but in the particular relationship "me-to-my-mother" and the responsibilities this one dictates for me. In the women's interview responses there was thus an emphasis on *particularity*, on the concrete details of a moral situation, as opposed to its universalizable or general features, which figure so prominently in mainstream ethical discourse.

Gilligan's initial conclusions from this research were tentative and carefully qualified; she emphasized that these differences had been detected via a rather quantitatively small study, that they could not be attributed to any "natural" gender difference in moral reasoning in view of the heavy socialization process by which gender differences are produced and maintained, and finally that some men have moral reasoning patterns which resemble those of the women studied.

But the excitement generated by her findings was intense. The strong emphasis on justice and impartiality in the original Kohlberg test was, after all, a prominent feature of much Western moral and political philosophy as well; we need only think of our brief excursion into the influential theory of Rawls above. Could it be that this way of thinking about ethics and social life is not gender-neutral but gendered and male? The possibility of a woman's ethic appeared, with a nudge from the empirical findings of Gilligan, and many feminist thinkers responded with enthusiasm.

At the same time, social scientists and feminist thinkers in other walks of life raised serious doubts about the Gilligan findings. Her sample was not only small but quite specific: It involved women considering an abortion, and it extended its study of them into the period following the abortion for those who had chosen the option. But this is a moral experience which men could not in all practicality share, so it is a moral situation in which difference would naturally emerge. Its exigencies are highly specific. Furthermore, some argued that Gilligan's interpretations of the subjects' responses went beyond what they had actually said and were mainly responsible for constituting the supposed gender differences in the first place.[18]

Nevertheless, the energetic pursuit of a "different voice" in ethics quickly took on a life of its own, becoming a theoretical rather than an empirically based enterprise. In addition to Gilligan's empirical study, Nel Noddings in her book *Caring: A Feminine Approach to Moral Education*[19] provided an analysis of moral life and a radical proposal for transforming the educational system, both of which were based on the immediate behavior of caring for relevant individuals. Gilligan's and Noddings' suggestive studies found a resonance with many women, who expressed a longstanding feeling that traditional ethical theories had always strangely seemed to alienate them, to lack something, and to reflect none of the ways in which they themselves think or feel they ought to think.

In philosophy, there emerged proposals for an "ethic of care," conceived as an alternative to the tradition's "ethic of justice."[20] In an ethic of care, the *relational self* which we have seen as an important element in much feminist thinking today is the basis for moral reasoning. The central directive of an ethic of care is that I should act always in such ways as to promote the well-being of both the others to whom I am in relation and the self which is relationally constituted. This is extremely vague as it stands, but the care approach in ethics accepts the vagueness of the theory's basis as a strength: Rules are less significant than a caring and attentive conscientious *presence* within one's moral situation, a sensitivity to the needs and desires of others, and a basic dispositional willingness to do what I can to create situations in which those needs can be met.

In her novel *The Nice and the Good*, Iris Murdoch places in the mind of a character who is facing death an eloquent statement of the ethic of care. The character, John Ducane, is a civil servant who has been appointed to investigate an apparent suicide in his bureau; in the course of the investigation, he has made discoveries about a colleague whom he intensely dislikes that give him considerable power over that person. He has spent a great deal of mental energy attempting to separate his duty from his desires. While trapped in a sea cave by a rising tide, he finally realizes what his course of action should be:

I wonder if this is the end, thought Ducane, and if so what it will all have amounted to. How tawdry and small it has all been. He saw himself now as a little rat, a busy little scurrying rat, seeking out its own little advantages and comforts. To live easily, to have cozy familiar pleasures, to be well thought of. . . . He thought, if I ever get out of here I will be no man's judge. Nothing is worth doing except to kill the little rat, not to judge, not to be superior, not to exercise power, not to seek, seek, seek. To love and to reconcile and to forgive, only this matters.

All power is sin and all law is frailty. Love is the only justice. Forgiveness, reconciliation, not law.[21]

Lest her readers dismiss this as the hysterical maunderings of a soul in
desperation, Murdoch shows in the concluding pages of the novel that
acting on this newfound moral insight brings peace, happiness, and
finally even intense romantic love to Ducane.

The abjuring of the egoistic self-oriented perspective, and of legalis-
tic and duty-based thinking, is typical of the ethic of care. Some feminist philosophers who admit the prima facie appeal of caring as a basic
moral disposition express reservations about the power of such a disposition to ground the whole of morality; don't we need robust concepts
of duty and obligation to cover those situations in which, for example,
we intensely dislike those we are involved with in some specific relationship? How can I realistically be expected to *care* about the Internal
Revenue Service, and make this my motive for paying my income tax,
when I contemplate the proportion of the federal budget that goes for
weapons stockpiling, nerve gas research, and other purposes foreign to
my personal values? Isn't it too stringent to require that, in addition to
tolerating and being civil, I must actually *care for* an obnoxious co-
worker who loses no opportunity to ridicule me to the head of my
department? I can recognize the saintliness of persons who have this
kind of flexible charity within their moral grasp, but I cannot feel that
morality requires it of everyone.

Rita Manning has argued that by distinguishing between two types of
care, caring for and caring about, we can begin to answer some of these
questions and meet the difficulties an ethic of care needs to meet if is to
be satisfying as a total moral vision.[22] Caring for typically involves
personal acquaintance in addition to some level of commitment to
assist the other's flourishing; it is interpersonal. Caring about, however, can be more distanced and can adapt itself to my other noninter-
personal values. Thus in the case of the obnoxious co-worker, an ethic
of care dictates that I should care *about* the working relationship
enough to hammer out some way of dealing with him—fondness and
direct ministrations are not a requirement. Joan Tronto also makes the

distinction between caring for and caring about, but to quite different purpose: She argues that, in our society, caring for is work that women do, while the more distanced caring about is the prerogative of men.[23] Tronto urges that a feminist ethic of care examine the gender implications of this division in kinds of caring, which will require an analysis of the social structures in which forms of caring are constructed and delegated.

Critics of the ethics of care are alarmed about the possibility that women's subordination is simply valorized and ratified by making caring a central moral directive.[24] There is something uncomfortably familiar about the vision of the caring, relating, attending moral agent who places others' needs in the center of her moral universe; she is the stereotypical female and we can effortlessly predict her lines: "Oh don't mind me!"; "Can I get you anything?"; "Is anything wrong?"; "Where does it hurt?"; "No I'm not busy"; "Wouldn't you like some more?"; and so forth.

There are really two criticisms inherent in this one. First, no feminist would want to advocate an ethic that endorses traditional prescriptions to subservience directed to any group that has been the recipient of such prescriptions to their detriment. In the South when I was growing up, during the 50s and early 60s, the distinction between a "good nigrah" and a "bad nigrah" was well known, although I never heard anyone spell it out in so many words: "good nigrahs" were those who were deferential, polite, subservient, hard-working, and self-effacing. There was also a certain way of saying, "She's a GOOOOD WOMAN" that carried the same connotations, especially regarding the willingness to work like a mule in the service of her husband and children. The ethic of care runs the danger of putting an ethical blessing on this kind of pernicious and privilege-serving evaluation.

Second, the ethic of care, in elevating a certain ideology of women's traditional behavior to the status of moral prescription, obscures women's violent and destructive capacities. Women are quite capable of performing some caring service and subsequently taking it out of the hides of the beneficiaries tenfold, either through low-grade but persistent psychological torture ("No one gives a hoot about little old me") or through more violent means such as child abuse. Attending to an ethic of care may obscure a realistic political analysis of the conditions causing and encouraging women's violence and self-destructive anger.

It may be that an ethic of care addresses something women both recognize about their own moral thinking and value and wish to preserve, but (a) such an ethic must be supplemented by a politically viable and central conception of justice; and (b) careful thought must be given to the question of precisely *what kind of society* needs to be constructed in order to ensure that the exploitative potential of the disposition to care does not take center stage. In what kind of world might caring be spontaneous, fulfilling, creative, joyous, and life-affirming for both the carer and the one cared for? In the next section we examine a care-based ethic in which, it is argued, a powerful world-transforming potential emerges logically from the activity of caring itself.

MATERNAL ETHICS

In a series of papers beginning in 1980 and culminating in the book *Maternal Thinking: Toward a Politics of Peace*,[25] feminist philosopher Sara Ruddick has developed an ethical and epistemological outlook based on the work of mothering. In many ways her project is related to the feminist-standpoint epistemologies we reviewed in the preceding chapter, for Ruddick begins with the premise that practices shape beliefs and give rise to the values which will in turn govern practices.[26] There is no essential connection between being a "mother"—a person who does maternal work—and being a *woman*, according to Ruddick. Men can do maternal work,[27] and women can refuse this work; however, historically, maternal work has been women's work and refusing to do it has had its costs for women. Ruddick is also aware that the conditions under which maternal work is and has been done display enormous variation, including economic, cultural, ethnic, and racial differences. Nevertheless she claims to have traced some very general and widely recurrent practices and modes of thought common to all who do this work.

What is maternal work, and how does it yield an ethic and a political vision? The practices of mothering center, of course, on nurturing and

preserving a child, making possible its physical and mental development from vulnerable babyhood or childhood to independent youth and
adulthood. This can be done well or badly, in conditions of comfort or
hardship, with greater or less "success." False and oppressive images
of "good mothers" and "bad mothers" produce guilt and anxiety in
those who struggle to do their maternal work as best they can under
their particular circumstances. Thus separating the spurious from the
genuine among the values generated by maternal practice is no small
task; and it is not made easier by the saccharine sentimentality with
which Western capitalist cultures have surrounded "motherhood" (*"M
is for the many things you gave me . . ."*).

But the central exigencies of child care generate some clear virtues,
recognizable even to those maternal workers who cannot or will not
exemplify the virtues. Ruddick argues that maternal work requires
both cognitive and moral attitudes whose sophistication and complex-
ity have gone unrecognized, largely because of the relegation of wom-
en's work to the domain of the "natural" (as we saw in Chapter Two).

A central organizing virtue of maternal work according to Ruddick's
analysis is "attentive love," the description of which is developed in
terms drawn from works of Simone Weil and Iris Murdoch:[28]

The concept "attentive love" which knits together maternal thinking, designates
a cognitive capacity—attention—and a virtue—love. It implies and rewards a
faith that love will not be destroyed by knowledge, that to the loving eye the lov-
able will be revealed.[29]

In maternal practice, the attention and the love mutually interpret one
another, so that the attention is not dispassionate nor is the love incapa-
ble of accurate observation. A mother must be able to see with "the
patient eye of love"[30] the person her child is and is becoming; attention
of this kind is "at once an act of knowing and an act of love."[31] "Attention lets difference emerge without searching for comforting common-
alities, dwells upon the *other*, and lets otherness be."[32]

This is clearly the kind of virtue one could exercise in contexts other
than mothering; in fact, it sounds appealing as a general way of inter-
acting with those close to us and in a qualified version would make a

morally attractive model for many human relations. This is part of the overall theme of Ruddick's work—that from a careful philosophical reflection on what ideals emerge from maternal thinking, we can glean moral lessons applicable in other walks of life. The absence of reflection in mainstream Western philosophy on the practices of mothers has meant impoverishment and distortion in the resultant ethical visions.

In the relationship between a mother and a child, a dialectic of control and "letting go" is constantly at work. The world is filled with dangers which threaten to horrify, traumatize, injure, or annihilate children. Yet children must and will learn to make their way alone in this same threatening world. Stifling overprotectiveness prevents them from learning, and excessive permissiveness or obliviousness to danger puts them at risk; both attitudes endanger their survival. Ruddick claims that mothers maintain a constant calculation and recalculation of balance between safety and risk, clutch and release, shielding and exposing, which requires of them a sensitivity to the environment and to human vulnerability which are also moral and cognitive virtues.[33] The child moves through this calculation process as a constantly changing variable whose moods, recent experiences, state of development, and present desires all must be factors of analysis; the child is an "open structure"[34] reaching across time; a mother's knowledge comprehends at once its helpless infancy, its history, and its future independence. Thus once again, as in Chapter Two, we have located a factor in many women's experiences of the world that defies rigid spatiotemporal boundaries. Those who do maternal work (mainly, but not necessarily, women) must live in a plurality of existential possibilities and be able to view the child as a plurality of selves.

The theme of maternal nonviolence is perhaps the most controversial of Ruddick's many controversial theses, however. Ruddick argues that there is a key feature of maternal work which centers on the discovery and development of nonviolent strategies: for conflict resolution, for nonoppressive control, for protection. The fact of violence *in* mothering is not to be denied. Mothers experience violent emotions both in the interests of and against the children they care for as well as the other adults who figure importantly in their practices.

Nevertheless, as Ruddick points out, a nonviolent strategy for overcoming even the most potentially violent conflicts is frequently employed. Mothers know that it is in the interests of their children and themselves to find ways out of conflict situations which do not provoke injury or destruction. In this light, maternal work can be seen to be "governed by ideals of nonviolence."[35] The conflict resolutions mothers must forge do not result in the parties going away from one another to live in distant lands or interact at a distance; they must all continue to live together or to interact in the same spaces as those in which the initial conflict occurred. Mothers must therefore learn to forge a "sturdy" peace, in which lively interests of all parties are served, in which all parties continue to feel enfranchised. Likewise in discipline, the child's interests must weigh heavily; ". . . [t]o the extent that a child is damaged, i.e. controlled violently, the ends of preservation and growth are compromised."[36] Of course, these ends do get compromised; the analysis here is of the ideals which govern the maternal practices, rather than average success rates of meeting those ideals.

Meditation on the ways in which maternal work is antithetical to violence, and on some recent political events in which mothers took effective stands against violent and repressive political regimes (e.g., the *Madres des Desaparecidos* of Argentina), brings Ruddick to the brink of a political vision:

A feminist maternal politics of peace: peacemakers create a communal suspicion of violence, a climate in which peace is desired, a way of living in which it is possible to learn and to practice nonviolent resistance and strategies of reconciliation. This description of peacemaking is a description of mothering.[37]

This vision is part imagination, part ethical ideal, and part historical reality. Ruddick hopes that a careful moral attention to the virtues which can emerge from maternal work will encourage the development of social structures which resemble the vision ever more closely. It is a bold and utopian vision, and none the less valuable for being so.

Criticisms of Ruddick's project have been numerous, and I will here mention only a few. Lorraine Code argues that in focusing so intensely on the personal elements of the maternal practices she describes, Ruddick mystifies by overlooking the *institutional* factors governing the production and pursuit of those practices.[38] Large-scale cultural forces, including the demands of a capitalistic economic system, the testimony of scientific "experts" in a variety of fields, medical practitioners, and government agencies all have a stake in shaping "motherhood" in certain not always compatible directions. In this vast network of constructive forces, the moral-cognitive efforts of individual mothers are but one small knot of energy. Code also maintains, as have several other critics, that Ruddick's analysis really fits best only a specific form of mothering: that prevalent in developed capitalist nations among middle-class heterosexual nuclear families.

Victoria Davion has recently argued that the pacifist potential of Ruddick's interpretation of mothering is at odds with the passionate attachment which can exist between mothers and children, and with the violence which mothers must be willing to threaten or engage in when their children are in danger. Classical pacifism, as exemplified by the teachings of Gandhi, whom Ruddick quotes with approval, is a resignation of passionate inner disturbance and of all violent interaction with others. Davion regards this attitude as untenable, undesirable from a feminist perspective (as encouraging a dangerous passivity) or from any other sensible point of view.

In spite of these criticisms, all of which seem well-taken and worthy of further thought, it should be said that Ruddick's work has had an inspiring and empowering effect for many who have read her essays or heard her speak. In my view, it constructs a valuable bridge between women's traditional practices of birthing and child-rearing and contemporary feminist ideals and aims. As thus forging connections among women, and as possibly grounding hope for a peaceful global future, it is an invaluable contribution to feminist philosophical thought.

LESBIAN ETHICS

We saw in Chapter One that lesbian feminist philosophers are committed to projects of radical rethinking of traditional topics and to designing ways of thinking which affirm, rather than render invisible or deny, the reality of alternatives to patriarchal heterosexuality. We now examine some of the work that has recently been done in the relatively new field of lesbian ethics.

Lesbian ethics consists of more or less systematic explorations of the moral problems and prospects which attend lesbian experience, though in many cases they seem highly relevant to nonlesbian feminist concerns as well. One of the most systematic and sustained contributions in this area is Sarah Lucia Hoagland's *Lesbian Ethics*, which attempts to develop an ethical vision designed specifically for the lesbian community.[39]

Hoagland believes that such a community is to a certain extent an *ideal* at the present time. While for many lesbians a network of friends is not only a source of support but also a necessity for survival, given the degree of intolerance they face in our culture, a true community goes beyond the fragmentary alliances formed in a subculture—it relies on deep connections and a sense of shared identity and interests which are as yet only partially realized.[40] It is in part to further the process of community-building that Hoagland offers her ethical project.

What obstacles exist to make such community-building a laborious and morally complex process? One of the central obstacles is a problematic dialectic between personal independence or autonomy and interpersonal bonding or connection-building. Any potential member of the lesbian community has had to exercise extraordinary individual strength and stubbornness in order to assert her identity while being inundated with heterosexual prescriptions. As Julia Penelope has written elsewhere, the lesbian has "a mind that must have its own integrity on its own terms." She continues:

We don't willingly submit to the dogmas of authority. Even when we try to hide our bad attitude from those who have power over us by retreating into silence, we stand out like dandelions in a well-manicured lawn. Lesbians are the weeds that blossom proudly, stubbornly, in heterosexual families; no matter what lethal methods they use to eradicate us, we keep springing back. We are resilient, and our roots go deep.[41]

The specific oppression the lesbian faces requires her to develop and maintain a degree of intellectual and moral autonomy which can make the formation of lasting community a perilous and difficult process. A group of persons, each of whom has a "mind that must have its own integrity on its own terms," will have to create its own model for connection and cohesion, and the task will not be a simple one.

Hoagland argues that existing models for group associations and communities within the dominant culture are affected by dominance and subordination relationships which may not always be readily apparent, but which are there nevertheless and render them useless for liberatory lesbian purposes.[42] In order for a truly ethical community to develop, Hoagland argues that we must develop a conception of the self which allows for autonomy and independence *in connection* and a revised conception of the virtues and values which will allow such a self in community to flourish. Both the conception of the self and the value system must be crafted in such a way as to keep at bay the pervasive configurations of dominance and subordination which have so unfortunately colored Western culture.

Hoagland gives up the term *autonomy* as hopelessly tinged with its philosophical history and invents a new term, *autokoenony*, to designate the central moral trait of the self-in-community.[43] Such a self will be bonded but not bound, depending but not dependent, strong but not controlling, and so forth. Hoagland clearly places at the center of her project a dialectic with which Western political philosophy has unsuccessfully struggled for quite some time—balancing individualistic and communalistic concerns. The key to her solution is constant vigilance against the insidious conceptual vocabulary of dominance/subordination. But she also emphasizes that the community and values to be created are importantly new and that the project *is* one of "creation" rather than transvaluating, which would mean merely changing nuances in the meaning of traditional values.

Referring to the increased visibility of lesbian existence in recent years, Hoagland writes:

The value which has emerged from this burst of lesbian be-ing, concomitant with the feminist movement and the gay liberation movement, lies in all we have created, particularly the reality of lesbian context, problematic though it also is. And focusing on lesbian integrity, moral integrity, and lesbian existence is key, I believe, to that value continuing to evolve from our choices.[44]

Hoagland believes that values emerge from the choices we make rather than that choices are made in accordance with pre-existing and independently justified values. This view has some background in existential philosophy, with its emphasis on the creation of the individual and of meaning in free and authentic acts. Hoagland's project differs decisively from those of existentialists, however, in that the creation of value which she envisions will be made in the interests of sustaining a definite specific community; it thus escapes the chilly individualism affecting much existentialist thought.

About the creativity of moral life as she envisions it, Hoagland writes: "The energy of [lesbian] creation involves not preservation and security, but risk and change. And an ethics appropriate to creativity, I believe, focuses on enabling our integrity and agency."[45]

The idea of developing an ethic for a specific community has seemed problematic to some. Does this mean that each human community should feel free to generate its own ethical code, to create values for itself? Does this mean that the Nazis could justify their actions by claiming that they are creating new value in the interests of preserving their (racist, oppressive, self-aggrandizing) community?

Hoagland might respond that her guiding assumption rules out the use of her moral method within any community which has dominance and subordination as its central logic, as did the Nazi "community." It is in order to distance herself as far as possible from this logic that she embarks on her ethical project in the first place. To attempt to apply its structure to grossly oppressive communities would be to subvert it from its purpose and sunder it from its basic ethical premise.

Marilyn Frye has expressed concern about the perceived need for an ethics within the lesbian community. She suggests that the preoccupation with "being good" is a legacy from an oppressive set of mechanisms for the control of women, designed to produce "dutiful daughters" and "submissive wives" and more generally a well-ordered hierarchical bureaucratic society in which the privileged are safely ensconced where they want to be. She approves of the radical potential of the idea of creating meaning and value but cautions against the genuineness of the need for a moral theory of anything like the traditional type in lesbian contexts.[46]

And Maria Lugones wonders how those lesbians who are members of plural identity-making communities (Latina, Angla, academic, lesbian in several different communities, etc.) can apply Hoagland's ethical vision to their lives. Lugones argues that the vision is crucially limited to fairly homogeneous and tightly knit communities which are growing; what then do we make of communities which are in immediate danger of disappearing, of communities among which we travel, feeling equal but distinct senses of ourselves as belonging members? She suggests that "we need to come to terms with a more complicated (multiplicitous) view of the self" and interpret the separation from patriarchal structures of dominance/subordination accordingly.[47]

My own view is that, while the complications surrounding the notion of "community" are considerable, Hoagland's conceptual apparatus is sufficiently flexible to permit the creation of multiple-community values. And the agenda she offers is fresh, radical, and a useful corrective to the age-old habits of dominance-thinking to which all of us fall prey in spite of our best efforts.

It should be clear from what has preceded that there is a tremendous amount of innovative thinking taking place in feminist ethics, both critical (as we saw in the case of Rawls and the liberal tradition) and constructive, as we have seen in our review of the ethics of care, maternal ethics, and lesbian ethics. Feminist ethics encourages us to dream of a world in which each individual is free, is valued, cares and is cared for, and has a strong sense of belonging. Feminist ethics then demands that we put our dreams to work, to build this "fairest city" somewhere in our neighborhood. Lorraine Code has suggested that we take hope from the fact that feminist interaction has already produced microcosmic communities which apply the liberatory political principles they cherish and make space for radically different, truly respectful, forms of human interaction.[48] Adherence to our ideals, combined with abundant energy, can help these small beginnings grow to greatness.

FOR FURTHER READING

Allen, Jeffner (ed.). *Lesbian Philosophies and Cultures*. Albany: SUNY Press, 1990.

Baier, Annette C. "What Do Women Want in a Moral Theory?;" *Nous* *19* (1985):53–63.

Bishop, Sharon. "Connections and Guilt;" *Hypatia 2* (1987):7–23.

Card, Claudia. "Lesbian Attitudes and *The Second Sex*;" *Hypatia 3* (1985):209–214.

Cole, Eve Browning, and Susan Coultrap-McQuin (eds.). *Explorations in Feminist Ethics: Theory and Practice*. Bloomington: Indiana University Press, 1992.

Friedman, Marilyn. "Feminism and Modern Friendship: Dislocating the Community," *Ethics 99* (1989): 275–290.

Green, Karen. "Rawls, Women, and the Priority of Liberty;" *Autralasian Journal of Philosophy,* supplementary volume 64 (1986):26–36.

Held, Virginia. "Birth and Death;" *Ethics 99* (1989):362–388.

Jaggar, Allison. "Feminist Ethics: Some Issues for the Nineties;" *Journal of Social Philosophy 20* (1989):91–107.

Kittay, Eva Feder, and Diana T. Meyers (eds.). *Women and Moral Theory*. Totowa, N.J.: Rowman & Littlefield, 1987.

Okin, Susan Moller. "Reason and Feeling in Thinking About Justice;" *Ethics 99* (1989):229–249.

Overall, Christine. "Heterosexuality and Feminist Theory;" *Canadian Journal of Philosophy 20* (1990):1–17.

Simons, Margaret. "Motherhood, Feminism, and Identity;" *Hypatia 2* (1984):349–359.

Trebilcot, Joyce. "Dyke Methods;" *Hypatia 2* (1988):1–13.

Trebilcot, Joyce (ed.). *Mothering: Essays in Feminist Theory*. Totowa, N.J.: Rowman & Allanheld, 1983.

CHAPTER SIX

CONCLUSION: CONVERGENCES AND CONTROVERSIES

Many projects within feminist philosophy have gone unmentioned in the preceding chapters, and I can only point to a few of these briefly before ending this book. Just as hardly any aspect of contemporary life has remained unchanged by the women's movement of the past three decades, so virtually no aspect of the traditional philosophy curriculum is untouched by feminist questioning and reshaping. It is my hope that the reader is well equipped by what we have surveyed so far to enter into any of the lively debates taking place in these diverse venues and to make a creative personal contribution to these debates.

In the fields of aesthetics or the philosophy of art, for example, feminist philosophers are working to appraise the definitions of "a work of art" which have been offered by mainstream aestheticians; they question the distinction between art and craft or handiwork and wonder whether it is a valid distinction given that women's traditional work seems to end up in the craft category, while that category bears a lesser status in the art world. Feminist aestheticians also examine the categories used in art criticism, with a view to discovering whether there are hidden or not-so-hidden agendas of elitism, racism, or sexism implicit in their structure or deployment.

In the philosophy of religion, feminists question the extent to which traditional theologies and religious institutions are objectionably male-centered, hierarchical, and devaluing of women. Since the pioneering radical feminist work of Mary Daly in this area,[1] critiques of religion and calls for a revitalized feminist spirituality have been numerous.

In the philosophy of science, important work has been done on the extent to which science can be considered gender-neutral (some of this work was mentioned in Chapter Four). In addition, feminist philosophers of science and scientists alike are working toward the creation of truly feminist scientific research environments and agendas; they observe that laboratories can be oppressive places, both for the lower-status workers within them (graduate students, lab assistants, etc.) and with regard to the societies that lie outside the laboratory walls. They work toward a humanized science, conscious of its responsibilities to the society that supports it, and willing to devote its energies to human liberation and human flourishing.

In biomedical ethics, feminist philosophers examine the extent to which women's health issues have been treated and discussed in different ways from men's, along with investigating the implications of reproductive technologies for women's autonomy and well-being. Some feminist medical ethicists advocate a revision of the entire concept of medical care, in the direction of more holistic understandings of human beings in their environments, rather than spot-diagnosis and crisis-response models of medicine.

These and many other areas are progressing and developing new critiques and new proposals for change, even as I write. And also as I write, feminist philosophers are embroiled in heated controversies about many issues which have deep and important implications. For example, there is widespread and painful awareness that feminist philosophy, like the Euro-American women's movement in general, has been justly accused of racism. Western philosophers, as we have seen, have tended to think and write as if people of color simply did not exist. Feminist philosophers have attempted not to follow along in this spuriously white discourse, but time and again covert exclusion and implicit racism have slipped into feminist philosophy. Thus there is a convergence of opinion as to both the necessity and the difficulty of eradicating a centuries-long tradition of racist thinking, but there is controversy about how this can be best accomplished. Sometimes this comes down to practical questions of what to include in a philosophy syllabus. For every voice of color introduced, some portion of the white male tradition must go. Some feel that this is acceptable, perhaps even an improvement; others worry about what important concept or fact the students may fail to learn from the dominant tradition. It *is* after all the dominant tradition, and some at least of its power is thoroughly deserved. But issues of course curriculum are perhaps largely symbolic, and indicative of the difficulty of accepting the charge of racism and exclusion at the deep level. More profoundly, when white feminists and black feminists engage in philosophical conversations, are the white feminists intellectually and/or morally entitled to *disagree* with the black feminists? To do so would seem in some ways presumptuous, but not to do so would seem like an abdication of one of philosophy's central activities—participation in meaningful and searching conversation about life's most complex matters.[2]

Another issue of both convergence and controversy concerns the relationship between lesbian feminist philosophy and nonlesbian feminist philosophy. There is a longstanding struggle in feminism generally surrounding the notion of "lesbian separatism." The term means different things to different people, but always connotes the idea of deliberate dissociation from males, male institutions, and "male-identified women." This struggle finds its counterpart within philosophy: should women-only philosophical conferences be held? Is the (almost entirely heterosexual) traditional philosophy canon still to be promoted as the core of a philosophy major? Is a lesbian philosopher required by intellectual responsibility to keep distant from heterosexually dominated institutions? Can heterosexual women (and men) really understand lesbian philosophies? And even if so, are they entitled to criticize them?

And also even as I write, a national conversation (conducted in rather irritated tones) is occurring about the issue of "political correctness," a confusing label now overlaid with emotional static and no longer clearly definable. In its early usage, political correctness seemed to denote the efforts to use inclusive language, avoid sexist terminology and practices, think in diversity-promoting terms, and the like—behaviors through which consciousness-raised people demonstrated their good will. It very quickly took on negative connotations of various kinds; to some it came to imply a merely formal kind of political propriety not rooted in deeply internal or sincere conviction. To others it brought with it associations of thought suppression, censorship, compulsory conformity to rules dictated by special-interest groups. Feminist philosophy has been involved in the correctness issue in all its phases, from the early earnest effort to *be* politically correct in the good sense to a more recent stage in which it has become the target of a kind of anticorrectness campaign. One can only hope that the heat of the rhetoric employed in the political-correctness debate will be accompanied by a corresponding amount of light shed on the real issue at stake: how to structure our thinking and our behavior in such ways as to produce a diverse, harmonious, and just human habitat.

While these controversial questions vary in their significance for the broader issues of feminist thought, they, like the questions about racism and separatism, are symptomatic of the struggle to honor difference while maintaining some sense of community and common cause. And this struggle is perhaps the central political struggle of our era. So, ultimately, it is a sign of growth and health that philosophical discussion about such difference-in-unity issues is taking place.

In this book we have seen that feminist philosophers are working on numerous projects both critical and constructive, designed both to enable us to understand the limitations of past philosophy and to transcend those limitations. We saw at the outset that one of the most central features of feminist philosophical method is its commitment to the inclusion of all thinkers in the construction and creation of philosophical understandings. No one knows better than a person who has been systematically excluded from an enterprise *both* how such exclusion feels *and* how the exclusion mechanisms work—at which precise points all but the privileged white men were quietly written out of philosophy's script. Thus, to forge a philosophy which is both inclusive and liberating for all is the prime directive in feminist thinking. Each reader must decide for herself or himself how this can best be done. To choose to be a non-participant, to keep silence, is to invite others to define us to ourselves. To choose not to take a position, as bell hooks reminds us, is also to take a position—namely, whatever position others choose for us.[3]

Philosophy has been many things in its long history: the shared wisdom of a nonliterate people, the avocation of a privileged and moneyed Greek male elite, the self-proclaimed "Queen of the Sciences," the charter of revolutions, the strange idiolect of certain eccentric Oxford dons, the private love of some, the "Absolute Unfolding Itself in Time," a meal ticket and badge of intellectuality for an academic few. Feminist philosophers wish that philosophy may now be an influence for freedom, for beauty, and for peace, and they are willing to work toward that transformation. bell hooks describes this work as a work of love:

That aspect of feminist revolution that calls women to love womanness, that calls men to resist dehumanizing concepts of masculinity, is an essential part of our struggle. It is the process by which we move from seeing ourselves as objects to acting as subjects. When women and men understand that working to eradicate patriarchal domination is a struggle rooted in the longing to make a world where everyone can live fully and freely, then we know our work to be a gesture of love. Let us draw upon that love to heighten our awareness, deepen our compassion, intensify our courage, and strengthen our commitment.[4]

Philosophy too can deserve our love and will blossom with our energy. Since, in the preceding pages of this book, we have had many occasions to observe philosophical doctrines laboring in the service of oppression and alternatively being crafted to serve the interests of freedom and humanity, the reader is well equipped to enter into feminist philosophy as a co-worker. In this vineyard the work has just begun, the controversies are rife, and the issues are confusing and constantly changing as new, formerly silenced voices are heard. But it is intensely rewarding work, and the harvest—a free and loving human future— may be sweet beyond our wildest expectations.

FOR FURTHER READING

Anzaldúa, Gloria (ed.). *Making Face, Making Soul/Haciendo Caras: Creative and Critical Perspectives of Women of Color.* San Francisco: Aunt Lute Foundation, 1990.

Frye, Marilyn. "On Being White: Toward a Feminist Understanding of Race and Race Supremacy;" *The Politics of Reality: Essays in Feminist Theory.* Freedom, Calif.: Crossing Press, 1983. Pp. 110–127.

Frye, Marilyn. "To Be and Be Seen: The Politics of Reality;" *The Poli-*

tics of Reality: Essays in Feminist Theory. Freedom, Calif.: Crossing Press, 1983. Pp. 152–174.

Hein, Hilda, and Carolyn Korsmeyer (guest eds.). *Hypatia: Journal of Feminist Philosophy* special issue on feminist aesthetics 5(2) (1990).

Holmes, Helen Bequaert, (guest ed.). *Hypatia: Journal of Feminist Philosophy* special issue on feminist ethics and medicine 4(2) (1989).

Narayan, Uma. "Working Together Across Difference: Some Considerations on Emotions and Political Practice;" *Hypatia: Journal of Feminist Philosophy* 3(2) (1988):31–47.

Narayan, Uma. "Poems;" *Hypatia: Journal of Feminist Philosophy* 3(2) (1988): 101–106.

Overall, Christine. *Ethics and Human Reproduction.* Boston: Allen & Unwin, 1987.

Purdy, Laura M. (guest ed.). Special issue of *Hypatia: Journal of Feminist Philosophy* on ethics and reproduction 4(3) (1989).

Spretnak, Charlene (ed.). *The Politics of Women's Spirituality.* Garden City, N.Y.: Anchor/Doubleday, 1983.

Tuana, Nancy (ed.). *Feminism and Science.* Bloomington: Indiana University Press, 1989.

Tuana, Nancy (guest ed.). *Hypatia: Journal of Feminist Philosophy* special issues on feminism and science 2(3) (1987) and 3(1) (1988).

NOTES

Chapter One

1. Aristotle, *Metaphysics* I.2, 982b12–16. W. D. Ross translates the relevant lines "For it is owing to their wonder that men both now begin and at first began to philoso-phize. . ." (*The Complete Works of Aristotle*, ed. Jonathan Barnes. Princeton, N.J.: Princeton University Press, 1984, p. 1554).
2. In saying that gender injustice is a constantly recurring feature of human societies, I do not mean to imply that its forms are uniform throughout time and across cultures or that all cultures display it in equal degree. On the contrary, the forms of gender inequality are dazzlingly various, and their degrees of intensity range along a wide spectrum.
3. For a clear and compelling discussion of the concept of oppression in feminist con-texts, see Marilyn Frye, "Oppression," in *The Politics of Reality: Essays in Feminist Theory* (Freedom, Calif.: Crossing Press, 1983), pp. 1–16.
4. For a brief discussion of Burke and Wollstonecraft and a good-sized excerpt from Wollstonecraft's *Vindication of the Rights of Woman*, see *Philosophy of Woman: An Anthology of Classic and Current Concepts*, 2nd ed., ed. Mary Briody Mahowald (Indi-anapolis: Hackett, 1983), pp. 203–220.
5. Wollstonecraft, *Vindication of the Rights of Woman*, in ibid., p. 208.
6. Ibid., p. 216.
7. John Stuart Mill, *On the Subjection of Women* (London: Chatto, 1869).
8. For a brief and very informative discussion of Wollstonecraft in the context of later suffragist and abolitionist feminism, see Carolyn Korsmeyer, "Reason and Morals in the Early Feminist Movement: Mary Wollstonecraft," in *Women and Philosophy: Toward a Theory of Liberation*, ed. Carol C. Gould and Marx W. Wartofsky (New York: Perigee/Putnam, 1980), pp. 97–111.
9. Originally serialized in Gilman's journal *The Forerunner* and not independently pub-lished, *Herland* was printed as a book for the first time in 1979 (New York: Pantheon).
10. Gilman, *Herland*, p. 7.
11. Ibid., p. 20.
12. Gilman influenced and was influenced by the American socialists of the late nineteenth century, among whom Edward Bellamy was prominent. Bellamy is relevant to our dis-cussion because he also wrote a popular utopian novel, *Looking Backward*, which would provide an interesting comparison and contrast to Gilman's. Bellamy's Utopia, though thoroughly socialist, is decidedly *not* feminist.

13. The professions of domestic laborer and child-care worker are overwhelmingly female. See *Facts on U.S. Working Women*, Fact Sheet No. 85–7, U.S. Department of Labor, July 1985.

14. See *Comparable Worth: An Analysis and Recommendations*, U.S. Commission on Civil Rights, June 1985.

15. Gilman, *Herland*, p. 79.

16. These articles were: J. R. Lucas, "Because You Are a Woman," *Philosophy* 48 (1973) 161–171; Sheila Ruth, "A Serious Look at Consciousness-Raising," *Social Theory and Practice* 2 (1973) 289–300; Abigail Rosenthal, "Feminism Without Contradictions," *Monist* 57 (1973) 28–42; Mary Mothersill, "Notes on Feminism," *Monist* 57 (1973) 105–114; and Eleanor Laudicina, "Toward New Forms of Liberation: A Mildly Utopian Proposal," *Social Theory and Practice* 2 (1973) 275–288.

17. Christine Pierce, "Equality: *Republic* V," *Monist* 57 (1973) 1–11.

18. For an account of how women involved in the civil rights and student activist movements came to realize that women's interests were not being well served by these political efforts and gradually separated from them to form women's groups as such, see Charlotte Bunch, *Passionate Politics*, (New York: St. Martin's Press, 1987), 1–45.

19. Thomas Nagel, "Sexual Perversion," *Journal of Philosophy* 66 (1969):5–17. Reprinted in Alan Soble, *Philosophy of Sex: Contemporary Readings* (Totowa, N.J.: Littlefield Adams & Co., 1980), 76–88.

20. For example, feminist philosopher Marilyn Frye concludes the introduction to her book *The Politics of Reality: Essays in Feminist Theory* with a frank statement about her own race, class, and professional privileges and limitations; subsequently in the book she frequently speaks of the particularities of her own experience and the ways in which these constitute possible sources of epistemological advantage or limitation. This accomplishes two important things: it reminds the reader of precisely who is speaking (thus dispelling the mystique of authority that surrounds the printed word in our culture), and it invites the reader to contribute her/his own perspective on the problems being addressed.

21. Diogenes Laertius, *Lives of the Philosophers* II.6–14 contains this and other evidences of Anaxagoras' unflappable outlook, all of which may be apocryphal. It is important to note only that we witness here an early contribution to the legend of the philosopher as unnaturally strong and serene.

22. Plato's *Crito* contains the conversation about our obligation to obey the law; the *Phaedo* contains the discussion of the immortality of the soul and concludes with a dramatic rendering of Socrates' own death.

23. Janice Moulton, "A Paradigm of Philosophy: The Adversary Method," in *Discovering Reality: Feminist Perspectives on Epistemology, Metaphysics, Methodology, and Philosophy of Science*, eds. Sandra Harding and Merrill B. Hintikka (Dordrecht: D. Reidel, 1983), pp. 139–148.

24. For example, American Indian students, whose traditional cultural views about speaking to one another and speaking in public are antithetical to the confrontational methods found in academic philosophy settings, tend to drop philosophy classes quickly if those classes employ the "Adversarial Paradigm."

Chapter Two

1. The concept of triple jeopardy is presented as a valuable tool for political analysis of the positions and problems of women of color in white-dominated societies by Beverly

Lindsay, "Minority Women in America: Black American, Native American, Chicana, and Asian American Women" in *The Study of Woman: Enlarging Perspectives of Social Reality*, ed. Eloise C. Snyder (New York: Harper & Row, 1979), pp. 318–363.

2. See Deborah K. King, "Multiple Jeopardy, Multiple Consciousness: The Context of a Black Feminist Ideology" (*Signs: Journal of Women in Culture and Society 14* (1988):42–72) for many specific examples requiring flexible-variable analysis of privilege.

3. Patricia Hill Collins, *Black Feminist Thought* (Boston: Unwin Hyman, 1990).

4. Ibid., p. 10. Collins' use of the phrase *subjugated knowledge* differs somewhat from that of Foucault, who originated it. (She explains the differences on p. 18, note 3.) Essentially, black women's knowledge is neither "naive" nor "localized" in the way that typical subjugated knowledges are for Foucault.

5. Ibid., p. 15.

6. Ibid., pp. 22–23 and Chapter 3, pp. 43–66.

7. Audre Lorde, "Litany for Survival," *The Black Unicorn* (New York: W. W. Norton, 1978), pp. 31–2.

8. Collins, pp. 73–75.

9. Ibid., pp. 76–77.

10. Ibid., p. 78.

11. Ibid.

12. See, for example, Patricia J. Williams, "On Being the Object of Property," *Signs: A Journal of Women in Culture and Society 14* (1988):pp. 5–24, for a creative exploration of the concept of personal identity based on reflections about slavery, invisibility, and the story-telling of black women family members.

13. Collins, pp. 119–123.

14. Ibid., p. 215. For a more detailed discussion of the ethics of care, see chapter III, sections 2 and 3.

15. Collins, p. 216.

16. Lorraine Code, *Epistemic Responsibility*. (Hanover, N.H.: University Press of New England, 1987).

17. Paula Gunn Allen, "How the West was Really Won," *The Sacred Hoop: Recovering the Feminine in American Indian Traditions* (Boston: Beacon Press, 1986), pp. 194–208.

18. See, for example, the essays "This Wilderness in My Blood: Spiritual Foundations of the Poetry of Five American Indian Women," "The Feminine Landscape of Leslie Marmon Silko's *Ceremony*," and "Kochinnenako in Academe: Three Approaches to Interpreting a Keres Indian Tale" Allen, *The Sacred Hoop*.

19. Allen, p. 2.

20. Paula Gunn Allen, "When Women Throw Down Bundles: Strong Women Make Strong Nations," describes with many concrete examples the ways in which white men set about destroying the women-centered structures of Indian culture, a process Allen equates with the attempted destruction of that culture itself. See Allen, pp. 30–42.

21. Gretchen Bataille and Kathleen M. Sands, *American Indian Women* (Lincoln: University of Nebraska Press, 1984), p. 48.

22. Allen, p. 17.

23. Joy Harjo, "For Alva Benson, and for All Those Who Have Learned to Speak," *That's What She Said*, ed. Rayna Green (Indianapolis: Indiana University Press, 1984), pp. 152–153.

24. Allen, p. 119.

25. There are two minuscule possible exceptions: Plato's *Symposium* does depict, in the

fantasy-speech of Aristophanes, primordial beings of all possible two-gender combinations including woman-woman; and Plato does call Sappho, the woman-loving poet of Lesbos, "the tenth muse." But nowhere is lesbian existence a philosophical subject in its own right.

26. Kate Millett, *Sexual Politics* (Garden City, N.Y.: Doubleday, 1969), pp. 470–471, n. 1. This passage is poignant testimony to the rapidity of the social changes which we have experienced in the last two decades; the "grudging tolerance" with which society regarded male homosexuality in 1969 has eroded, while the "issue" of "female homosexuality" is now very much alive.

27. Joyce Trebilcot discusses this kind of objection to her own radical epistemology in "Dyke Methods," *Hypatia: A Journal of Feminist Philosophy* 3(2) (1988):1–13; see pp. 12–13 especially.

28. Joyce Trebilcot, "More Dyke Methods," *Hypatia: A Journal of Feminist Philosophy* 5(1) (1990):140.

29. Jeffner Allen, "Poetic Politics: How the Amazons Took the Acropolis," *Hypatia: A Journal of Feminist Philosophy* 3(2) (1988):107–122.

30. Marilyn Frye, "In and Out of Harm's Way: Arrogance and Love," *The Politics of Reality: Essays in Feminist Theory* (Freedom, Calif.: The Crossing Press, 1983), pp. 53–83.

31. Ibid., pp. 81–82.

32. Alice Walker, "Am I Blue?," in Irene Zahava, *Through Other Eyes: Animal Stories by Women* (Freedom, Calif.: Crossing Press, 1988), pp. 1–6.

33. This is a very frequent theme in feminist ecological philosophy; for a clear and comprehensive recent treatment focusing on animal rights, see Josephine Donovan's "Animal Rights and Feminist Theory," *Signs: Journal of Women in Culture and Society* 15 (1990):350–375.

34. A very comprehensive survey of the woman-nature theme (including assimilations of women to various nonhuman animals) is Susan Griffin, *Woman and Nature: The Roaring Inside Her* (San Francisco: Harper & Row, 1978).

35. Val Plumwood, "Nature, Self, and Gender: Feminism, Environmental Philosophy, and the Critique of Rationalism," *Hypatia* 6 (1991):3–27.

36. Ibid., 5.

37. Ibid., 8.

38. Ibid., 8.

39. This point and a detailed critique of such applications can be found in Deborah Slicer, "Your Daughter or Your Dog? A Feminist Assessment of the Animal Research Issue," *Hypatia* 6 (1991):108–124.

40. Peter Singer, "Animal Liberation," *The New York Review of Books*, April 5, 1973.

41. Slicer, "Your Daughter or Your Dog?.." 115–116.

42. Karen Warren, "The Power and Promise of Ecological Feminism," *Environmental Ethics* 12 (1990):128.

Chapter Three

1. The remark about women appears in a letter to Vatier written in 1638; it is cited and discussed by Genevieve Lloyd, *The Man of Reason": "Male" and "Female" in Western Philosophy* (Minneapolis: University of Minnesota Press, 1984), p. 44.

2. *The Philosophical Works of Descartes*, translated by Elizabeth S. Haldane and G.R.T. Ross (2 volumes). (London: Cambridge University Press, 1973), p. 144. All citations of Descartes are from this edition.

3. "First philosophy" translates the Latin *prima Philosophia*, the standard scholastic des-

ignation for metaphysics and especially theology. It derives from Aristotle's *prote philosophia*, by which he designated the highest branch of philosophy, at once its most abstract and most fundamental form.

4. Descartes, Meditation 1, p. 144.
5. Meditation 1, p. 145.
6. Kathryn Pyne Addelson and Elizabeth Potter discuss this "epistemological individualism" as a feature of positivistic science and philosophy in "Making Knowledge," Addelson's *Impure Thoughts: Essays on Philosophy, Feminism, and Ethics* (Philadelphia: Temple University Press, 1991), pp. 221–238.
7. For further discussion of Descartes' project from a feminist perspective, see Susan Bordo, "The Cartesian Masculinization of Thought," *Signs: Journal of Women in Culture and Society 11* (1986): pp. 439–456.
8. Descartes, *Meditations*, tr. Elizabeth S. Haldane and G.R.T. Ross (London: Cambridge University Press, 1973), p. 148.
9. A thoughtful and compelling critique of Descartes' view of the self is given by Annette Baier, "Cartesian Persons," *Philosophia 10* (1981):169–188; reprinted in Baier's *Postures of the Mind: Essays in Mind and Morals* (Minneapolis: University of Minnesota Press, 1985), pp. 74–92.
10. *Plato: The Collected Dialogues*, ed. Edith Hamilton and Huntington Cairns (Princeton, N.J.: Princeton University Press, 1961), p. 62.
11. H. H. Price, "Our Evidence for the Existence of Other Minds," *Essays on Other Minds*, ed. Thomas O. Buford. (Urbana: University of Illinois Press, 1970), p. 140.
12. Ibid., pp. 140–141.
13. Ibid., p. 141.
14. Caroline Whitbeck, "A Different Reality: Feminist Ontology," pp. 64–88 *Beyond Domination: New Perspectives on Women and Philosophy*, ed. Carol C. Gould (Totowa, N.J.: Rowman & Allanheld, 1983), pp. 64–88; Lorraine Code, "Second Persons," *What Can She Know? Feminist Theory and the Construction of Knowledge* (Ithaca, N.Y.: Cornell University Press, 1991), Chapter 3 (pp. 71–109).
15. Paula Gunn Allen, "Who Is Your Mother? Red Roots of White Feminism;" *The Sacred Hoop: Recovering the Feminine in American Indian Traditions* (Boston: Beacon Press, 1986), pp. 209–221.
16. For another way of connecting dualism to the problem of other minds and a feminist critique of both, see Caroline Whitbeck, "Afterword to 'The Maternal Instinct,'" *Mothering: Essays in Feminist Theory*, ed. Joyce Trebilcot (Totowa, N.J.: Rowman & Allanheld, 1983.)
17. See Nancy Chodorow, "Family Structure and Feminine Personality," *Woman, Culture, and Society,* ed. Michelle Rosaldo and Louise Lamphere (Stanford, Calif.: Stanford University Press, 1974) pp. 43–57. See also Dorothy Dinnerstein, *The Mermaid and the Minotaur* (New York: Harper & Row, 1976).
18. Sigmund Freud, "On Femininity;" *New Introductory Lectures in Psychoanalysis*, ed. James Strachey (New York: W. W. Norton, 1965).
19. See in this regard Susan R. Bordo, "The Body and the Reproduction of Femininity: A Feminist Appropriation of Foucault;" *Gender/Body/Knowledge: Feminist Reconstructions of Being and Knowing*, ed. Alison M. Jaggar and Susan R. Bordo (New Brunswick, N.J.: Rutgers University Press, 1989), pp. 13–33.
20. A fascinating and disturbing study of the extent to which feminist thinking has been unconsciously race- and class-biased is Elizabeth V. Spelman's *Inessential Woman: Problems of Exclusion in Feminist Thought* (Boston: Beacon Press, 1988).
21. See the fascinating study by Donna Haraway, *Primate Visions: Gender, Race, and*

Nature in the World of Modern Science (New York: Routledge, 1989), which analyzes the ways in which sexism, racism, and speciesism intersected to construct the modern science of primatology. Primate "colonies," whether natural or artificially created, were interpreted in categories stemming from colonial thinking about native populations in third-world countries and their "social organization" thoroughly misdescribed in terms of male dominance and female submission.

22. *Proceedings and Addresses of the American Philosophical Association 63* (1990):62–63.
23. On this dynamic of physicality, male sexual aggression, and self-loathing see Murial Dimen, "Power, Sexuality, and Intimacy," *Gender/Body/Knowledge*, ed. Alison M. Jaggar and Susan R. Bordo (New Brunswick, N.J.: Rutgers University Press, 1989), pp. 34–51.
24. Luce Irigaray, "This Sex Which Is Not One," *New French Feminisms*, ed. Elaine Marks and Isabel de Courtivron (New York: Schocken, 1981).
25. Iris Marion Young, "Pregnant Embodiment: Subjectivity and Alienation," *Journal of Medicine and Philosophy 9* (1984):45–62; reprinted in Young's *Throwing Like a Girl and Other Essays in Feminist Philosophy and Social Theory* (Bloomington: Indiana University Press, 1990), pp. 160–176.

Chapter Four

1. G. H. Hardy, *A Mathematician's Apology* (London: Chatto & Windus, 1940).
2. Stephen Jay Gould, *Wonderful Life: The Burgess Shale and the Nature of History* (New York: W. W. Norton, 1989), p. 281.
3. For a critique of the concept of the expert, see Kathryn Pyne Addelson, "The Man of Professional Wisdom," *Discovering Reality: Feminist Perspectives on Epistemology, Metaphysics, Methodology, and Philosophy of Science*, ed. Sandra Harding and Merrill B. Hintikka (Dordrecht: Reidel, 1983), pp. 165–186.
4. Trinh T. Minh-ha, *Woman, Native, Other* (Bloomington: Indiana University Press, 1989), p. 58. Trinh's indictment of anthropology appears in Chapter II, "The Language of Nativism: Anthropology as a Scientific Conversation of Man with Man," pp. 47–78.
5. Ibid., p. 60.
6. Ibid., p. 67.
7. Evelyn Fox Keller, "Gender and Science," *Discovering Reality*, p. 192.
8. Michelle Le Doeuff, "Women and Philosophy," *French Feminist Thought*, ed. Toril Moi (Oxford: Basil Blackwell, 1987), p. 207.
9. Lorraine Code, *What Can She Know? Feminist Theory and the Construction of Knowledge* (Ithaca, N.Y.: Cornell University Press, 1991), p. 266.
10. Code discusses the implications of class privilege for epistemological advantage throughout *What Can She Know*; this is the fullest treatment of these issues to date in feminist epistemology.
11. Sandra Harding, *Whose Science? Whose Knowledge?* (Ithaca, N.Y.: Cornell University Press, 1991), pp. 112–117. Harding does not ultimately endorse feminist empiricism for this reason, but she does maintain that this institutional acceptability is one of its real strengths.
12. Alison M. Jaggar, *Feminist Politics and Human Nature* (Totowa, N.J.: Rowman & Allanheld, 1983), p. 356.
13. Lynn Hankinson Nelson, *Who Knows: From Quine to a Feminist Empiricism* (Philadelphia: Temple University Press, 1990).
14. Harding, *Whose Science? Whose Knowledge?*, p. 116.

15. The excellent fact-filled prefaces to each article in Robin Morgan's *Sisterhood Is Global* drive home this point about women's dual work roles as a virtual constant across the face of the earth.
16. See Nancy Hartsock, "The Feminist Standpoint: Developing the Ground for a Specifically Feminist Historical Materialism," *Discovering Reality*, pp. 283–310, for a sophisticated Marxian account of the economic dynamics of women's work/men's work, public and private, leading to a standpoint epistemology.
17. Terry Winant calls this "fluency in more than one set of discursive practices" and considers it the "epistemic consolation-prize" of being members of the dominated group; see "The Feminist Standpoint: A Matter of Language," *Hypatia 2* (1987): 123–148.
18. A clear and concise statement of the advantages of the feminist standpoint is made by Sandra Harding, "Starting Thought from Women's Lives: Eight Resources for Maximizing Objectivity," *Journal of Social Philosophy 21* (1990):140–149.
19. For a rather more cautionary picture of the potential consequences of inhabiting dual frameworks, see Uma Narayan, "The Project of Feminist Epistemology: Perspectives from a Nonwestern Feminist," *Gender/Body/Knowledge*, eds. Jaggar and Bordo, especially the conclusion, pp. 265–268.
20. Terry Winant discusses this difficulty, and offers an intriguing resolution using ideas drawn from the work of Hannah Arendt, in "The Feminist Standpoint: A Matter of Language."
21. See Claudia Card, "Gender and Moral Luck," *Identity, Character, and Morality: Essays in Moral Psychology*, ed. Amelie Oksenberg Rorty and Owen Flanagan (Cambridge, Mass.: MIT Press, 1990), pp. 199–218.
22. Jane Flax, "Postmodernism and Gender Relations in Feminist Theory," *Feminism/Postmodernism*, ed. Linda Nicholson (New York: Routledge, 1990), pp. 39–62.
23. Ibid., pp. 47–48, note 3.
24. Elspeth Probyn, "Travels in the Post-modern: Making Sense of the Local," *Feminism/Postmodernism*, pp. 176–189.
25. For a discussion of this notion of localized practical legitimation and its derivation from the thinking of Jean-François Lyotard, see Nancy Fraser and Linda Nicholson, "Social Criticism Without Philosophy," *Feminism/Postmodernism* pp. 19–38.
26. See Charlene Haddock Seigfried, "Where Are All the Pragmatist Feminists?," *Hypatia 6* (1991):1–20.
27. See Nancy Hartsock, "Rethinking Modernism," *Cultural Critique 7* (1987):187–206, for a critique of postmodernism as potentially imperialistic, denying the validity of third-world voices in struggle.
28. Sandra Harding, *Feminism and Methodology* (Bloomington: Indiana University Press, 1987), p. 189.
29. See also Uma Narayan, "The Project of Feminist Epistemology," especially pp. 260–261, for an analogous concern.
30. Jane Flax, "Postmodern Feminism and Gender Relations," pp. 56–57.

Chapter Five

1. John Rawls, *A Theory of Justice* (Cambridge, Mass.: Harvard University Press, 1971).
2. Ibid., p. 11, note 4.
3. Ibid., p. 12.
4. John Rawls, "Fairness to Goodness," *Philosophical Review 84* (1975).
5. Susan Moller Okin, "John Rawls: Justice as Fairness—For Whom?," *Feminist Inter-*

pretations and Political Theory, ed. Mary Lyndon Shanley and Carole Pateman (University Park, Pa.: Penn State University Press, 1991), pp. 181–198.

6. Okin, op.cit.; Annette Baier, "What Do Women Want in a Moral Theory?," *Nous 19* (1985):53–63; Seyla Benhabib, "The Generalized and the Concrete Other;" *Feminism as Critique*, ed. Seyla Benhabib and Drucilla Cornell (Minneapolis: University of Minnesota Press, 1987), pp. 77–95.

7. Annette Baier, in the article cited in note 6, stresses the importance of a basic commitment to honesty in the original position and points out that Rawls really has no way to account for this aspect of his thought experiment. Baier connects this to a general inattention to the richness of the moral training which mothers pass along to their children, an inattention found not only in Rawls but rife throughout the liberal tradition.

8. Rawls, *Theory of Justice*, p. 491.

9. Ibid., p. 490.

10. Okin, pp. 185–186 and passim.

11. Rawls, pp. 128–129.

12. Rawls' adherence to this detail about the original-position holders, that they may be thought of as "heads of families," is not as strong as some of his critics have claimed. Okin, for example, thinks he is really insistent upon it; but Rawls only says that this provides one way of ensuring that each member of the next generation will have someone who cares about their interests. It still remains interesting that biological parenthood is the *only* basis that comes to Rawls' mind for concern for the next generation.

13. Rawls, p. 128 and passim.

14. Ibid., pp. 490–491.

15. Okin argues, however, that Rawls' vision of the "original position" has really revolutionary feminist potential, in that a more careful application of the thought experiment could lead us to challenge "the gender structure" and to think critically about how to achieve justice within the family; see pp. 190–196 of her article.

16. Lawrence Kohlberg, *Collected Papers on Moral Development and Moral Education*; Moral Education Research Foundation, Harvard University, 1973.

17. Carol Gilligan, *In a Different Voice; Psychological Theory and Women's Development* (Cambridge: Harvard University Press, 1982).

18. See, for example, the forum discussion of Gilligan's findings which appeared in *Signs: Journal of Women in Culture and Society 11* (1986):304–333. The anthology *Women and Moral Theory*, edited by Eva Feder Kittay and Diana T. Meyers (Totowa, N.J.: Rowman & Littlefield, 1987), consists of essays critically discussing aspects of the Kohlberg–Gilligan controversy.

19. Nel Noddings, *Caring: A Feminine Approach to Ethics and Moral Education* (Berkeley: University of California Press, 1984).

20. See, for example, the anthology *Explorations in Feminist Ethics: Theory and Practice*, ed. Eve Browning Cole and Susan Coultrap-McQuin (Bloomington: Indiana University Press, 1992) in which papers by Rita Manning, Dianne Romain, Roger Rigterink, Julie Ward, and others debate a care ethic.

21. Iris Murdoch, *The Nice and the Good* (New York: Viking Press, 1968), p. 329.

22. Rita Manning, "Just Caring," *Explorations in Feminist Ethics*, 45–54.

23. Joan C. Tronto, "Women and Caring: What Can Feminists Learn About Morality from Caring?;" *Gender/Body/Knowledge*, ed. Jaggar and Bordo, pp. 172–187.

24. See, for example, the articles by Claudia Card, Sarah Lucia Hoagland, and Barbara Houston that constitute a review symposium of Nel Noddings' *Caring* in *Hypatia 5* (1990):101–119, along with Noddings' response in the same volume (pp. 120–126). Card argues that Noddings has no viable account of our moral relations to distant and

unknown persons; Card and Hoagland both argue that the ethic of care, at least as Noddings presents it, threatens to perpetuate and obscure exploitative relationships; and Houston maintains that an ethic of care cannot suffice to ground morality.

25. Sara Ruddick, *Maternal Thinking: Toward a Politics of Peace* (New York: Ballantine Books, 1989).
26. Ruddick discusses feminist-standpoint epistemologies, and diverges from them on one critical point, in the Introduction to Part III of her book, pp. 127–140. She does not agree that the feminist standpoint should be granted a lasting position of epistemological privilege but argues for a pluralism of standpoints.
27. Ruddick stretches ordinary usage so far as to claim that men can be mothers; in what follows I will adhere to her use of the term *mother* in this extended sense, though the difficulty of reading the term *mother* as male-inclusive is considerable, and probably instructive.
28. Ruddick, pp. 119–123.
29. Ibid., pp. 119–120.
30. Ruddick is here quoting Iris Murdoch, *The Sovereignty of Good* (New York: Schocken, 1971), p. 40.
31. Ruddick, p. 120.
32. Ibid., p. 122.
33. Ibid., pp. 72–73, for example, though this is a recurring theme of the book.
34. Ibid., p. 96.
35. Ibid., p. 161.
36. Ibid., p. 171.
37. Ibid., p. 244.
38. Lorraine Code, *What Can She Know? Feminist Theory and the Construction of Knowledge* (Ithaca, N.Y.: Cornell University Press, 1991), pp. 88–95.
39. Sarah Lucia Hoagland, *Lesbian Ethics: Toward New Value* (Palo Alto, Calif.: Institute of Lesbian Studies, 1988).
40. Hoagland, pp. 145–149. For the distinction between community and subculture Hoagland quotes Julia Penelope (Stanley), "Lesbian Relationships and the Vision of Community," *Feminary 9* (1978).
41. Julia Penelope, "The Lesbian Perspective," *Lesbian Philosophies and Cultures*, ed. Jeffner Allen (Albany: SUNY Press, 1990), p. 90.
42. Hoagland, Chapter 1 ("Separating from Heterosexualism" presents the argument concerning the pervasiveness of dominance/subordination in heterosexual culture.
43. The term *autokeonony* is a combination of the Greek prefix *auto*, meaning "self," with the Greek term for "community" or "sharing," *koinonia*.
44. Hoagland, p. 291.
45. Ibid., pp. 291–292.
46. Marilyn Frye, "A Response to *Lesbian Ethics*," *Hypatia 5* (1990); 132–137.
47. Maria Lugones, "Hispaneando y Lesbiando: On Sarah Hoagland's *Lesbian Ethics*," *Hypatia 5* (1990); 138–146.
48. Lorraine Code, *What Can She Know?*, p. 292.

Chapter Six

1. Mary Daly, *Beyond God the Father: Toward a Philosophy of Women's Liberation* (Boston: Beacon Press, 1973).
2. An anthology absolutely filled with wonderful material about issues uniting and dividing feminists on the subject of color difference is Gloria Anzaldúa (ed.), *Making Face,*

Making Soul/Haciendo Caras: Creative and Critical Perspectives by Women of Color (San Francisco: Aunt Lute Foundation, 1990).
3. bell hooks, "'When I was a Young Soldier for the Revolution': Coming to Voice," *Talking Back* (Boston: South End Press, 1989), pp. 10–18.
4. bell hooks, "Feminism: A Transformational Politic," ibid., pp. 26–27.

INDEX